This is the part where you're supposed to have reviews from well-known people who recommend your book. Since I've never written anything else before, feel uncomfortable even calling myself an author, and am completely unknown in the book world, I'll give you the three reviews I have so far. They're totally unbiased.

It's very, very, very good.

—*My dad, Jim*

My eyes were the first to see this book. I'm pretty sure it was just because Nicole knew I would be the most critical. I totally want to make fun of her for being an "author." All I can say is wow. I didn't want to, but I loved it. It's so relatable. Especially for someone like me, who is not as passionate about this topic as Nicole is. It's starting to make me see things differently—like maybe Nicole kind of knows what she's talking about.

—*My sister, Ashley*

You brought me (in three reading hours) what ten years of Catholic school didn't. I'm in love with your chapters, and I feel like I'm renewed enough to get back to relying on God. I grew up with a confidence that I was loved on a different level than an earthly level, but I didn't really know what that meant. At all. Your examples throughout the chapters connect the dots in a way that God spoke right through you! I laughed out loud multiple times. I was sad when I ran out of pages to read. You're one talented person. Wow. I *love* your book. It's special—very special. It's a calling. I hope the whole world reads your thoughts. Thank you because I feel honored to have read what I have read so far.

—*My friend, Lyndsay*

CURSED WITH COMMON SENSE

HOW I REALIZED THINKING YOU'RE TOO SMART FOR GOD IS REALLY DUMB

NICOLE NELSON

WESTBOW
PRESS®
A DIVISION OF THOMAS NELSON
& ZONDERVAN

WestBow Press books may be ordered through booksellers or by contacting:

WestBow Press
A Division of Thomas Nelson & Zondervan
1663 Liberty Drive
Bloomington, IN 47403
www.westbowpress.com
1 (866) 928-1240

This book is a work of non-fiction. Unless otherwise noted, the author and the publisher make no explicit guarantees as to the accuracy of the information contained in this book and in some cases, names of people and places have been altered to protect their privacy.

ISBN: 978-1-9736-5956-3 (sc)
ISBN: 978-1-9736-5955-6 (hc)
ISBN: 978-1-9736-5957-0 (e)

Library of Congress Control Number: 2019904813

Print information available on the last page.

WestBow Press rev. date: 5/2/2019

To Eric, Austin, and Brynn. You guys are the inspiration for everything I do. I love you more than I can ever express.

A big thank-you to Eagle Brook Church. Thank you for opening my eyes and teaching about Jesus in a way that finally made sense to me.

CONTENTS

CONTENTS

INTRODUCTION

I hope the title of this book doesn't imply that I'm just oozing with common sense. I didn't realize "jukebox" wasn't called a "jutebox" until I was thirty-five years old. I only now know it's jukebox because somehow last year, my TV got switched to closed captioning, and for weeks, I couldn't figure out how to undo it. One night I was watching Jimmy Fallon, and they were talking about "juteboxes."

Why are they spelling it with a K? It's not jukebox—it's jutebox. I thought closed captioning had spelled it wrong. I googled it and realized I was the one who was wrong. A person overflowing with common sense would have known how to spell that. And how to get closed captioning off the TV.

For some reason, though, when the topic of God or Jesus came up, I thought I had too much common sense, or was too independent to believe it. I was way smarter than most of those naive people who actually believed in God. I thought Christianity was far below someone of my intelligence. I asked people their reasons for believing, and they'd say that they'd just always believed. That answer didn't make sense.

It felt as if nobody understood my struggle. Getting help with my unbelief was like trying to get help with losing weight, only it's obvious the person giving the advice has always just naturally been in shape. They think they've discovered some big secret that will help you, but you know they've never been more than ten pounds from their goal weight.

You nod and listen to them talk about their "struggle" to get in shape, but their before and after pictures look pretty much the same. *Aren't they just standing in better lighting for their after?* As they're telling you about their workout or favorite protein shake, you want to shout, "You don't get it! You don't understand what it really means to struggle with your weight. I don't think we're on the same page when we say *struggle*."

It's hard to listen to someone who can't understand where you're coming from. It would be more helpful to get advice from someone whose before picture is dramatically different from their after. Someone who wasn't just born like that. Someone who had to fight for their results.

That's how I felt about faith and Christianity. I was getting advice from people who told me, "I've just always believed." If I expressed doubts in God, they told me to read a verse in the Bible to help ease my doubt.

I wanted to shout, "You don't get it! You don't know what it means to struggle with your faith. I don't even know if I believe the Bible." It would be more helpful to get advice and guidance from someone whose life before God was dramatically different from someone who has just always believed—someone who knows the struggle.

If you've ever felt like that with your faith, then it's your lucky day. I'm your "out-of-shape" friend. My before picture is dramatically different from my after. I didn't just "always believe." This has been a struggle. I'm the person who spent most of her life trying to cut corners, and I thought there was another way to find joy and purpose outside of God. I didn't want to conform to the way I viewed Christianity and other Christians. I fought this every step of the way.

Some people will read my journey and wonder how I could have been so out of shape. Things that I find profound will seem like common knowledge to them. They might read this and wonder how I didn't *just know* some of this stuff. They may even feel sorry for me that I was so far off in the direction my life was going.

These people are like the skinny, in-shape people with the perfect outfits who spend more time at the gym taking selfies than actually working out. I'm the one in an old T-shirt, gasping for breath and sweating over all of the equipment. I definitely don't want my picture taken. I want to punch the skinny girl in the face because I'm both annoyed and jealous that this seems to come so naturally for her. I look at her and wonder, *How is this so easy for you? It's like you don't even have to try.* This book might be fun for these people to read to see how I was so far off. Maybe it can help them see what it's like to be searching, questioning, and not just born with faith.

I want "church people" to know what it feels like to be a "non-church person." I would like the church people to have a better understanding of how they sound to non-church people. I want non-church people to know what it feels like to be a church person. I would like non-church people to know that most church people are a lot smarter than you think. Most are not just believing because their parents told them to. They aren't just off in their own make-believe world. Okay? Okay. This stuff is good for all of us to know.

This book is mostly for the out-of-shape person who's struggling to believe, for the person who knows there's more to life but is not sure what it is. The problem is usually that type of person isn't interested in reading a book about faith. They're sitting on the couch, perfectly happy watching Netflix and eating chips. Why would you work out when it's so much easier to sit on the couch?

That was me for most of my life. *Why are people so into church and God? Do they not have common sense? What's the big deal? There's no way it's real, and if it is, I'm not interested. It's not worth the effort. Thanks, but, no, thanks. I'm fine with what I'm doing. Get out of my business.*

If that's you, here's my plan. I'm going to try to get you interested in the beginning with my stories of my "before." Maybe you'll find them relatable or funny or maybe sad. Maybe you'll find yourself in those parts of my story. Please stick with me (especially through chapters 5 and 6, because that's where I would've quit reading during my before), because I really want you to read the full story. I didn't become as weird as you may think. Or maybe I did. I'm not really sure anymore.

If things are going really well for you right now, you won't have a strong desire to read this book. It's easy to rely on only yourself when things are good. You think God is more for desperate people. Sometimes things need to fall apart in order to have the desire to change your ways.

Things had to fall apart for me. It was like I was living in a house where the foundation was crumbling. I kept trying to fix it by painting the bathroom a new color or getting a new picture for the walls. These things seemed easier than dealing with the real problem in my life. I knew something major was wrong, but fixing the foundation was too hard. I just kept decorating, hoping that would distract from the giant hole in my life. It's not that I didn't want it fixed; it's just that it seemed too hard to redo my whole life. Besides that, I didn't even know where to start. I just kept getting more home décor, hoping to distract myself into thinking things were good enough. At the very least, I would look good to people who didn't know what was really going on. I wanted my life to be different—better—from the foundation up. Some people told me I needed Jesus to be the foundation that my life was built on, but I didn't know how Jesus was going to help much (if He was even real).

When the idea to write a book popped into my head one day, I quickly shut it down. *What business do I have writing a book? I would have no idea how to do that.* I'm proud to say I have always known the difference between *their, there,* and *they're.* I get a little thrill when I see someone use *to, too,* and *two* correctly, but that's as far as I would go in saying I'm qualified to write.

Before I even realized I was going to write a book, I started writing some of this stuff down in the notes section of my phone. Whenever I was bothered by some sort of issue, I contemplated it in my head for days, and then all of a sudden, I had this urge to write it out. All of these words were suddenly ready to come out and summarize what had been on my mind. When the words came, they felt urgent, as though I couldn't get them out fast enough. A lot of times it was while I was in the middle of drying my hair. I had to stop and write with a half wet head. After I was done writing, I went over what I'd just written, and usually thought it actually made sense. I then was able to stop thinking about whatever it was that had been on my mind. I remember wondering why I was writing all of this stuff down, and I didn't have an answer. I felt I just had to do it.

After I'd gotten used to the idea that I wanted to turn this all into a book, I was all in. I went to a writer's conference to see if there was some sort of magic way to write a book that everyone else knew about except for me. Turns out there wasn't a set way to do this, which was both a relief and a terror. I had to make this up as I went.

This book is a collection of all the notes and stories that I've been wrestling with for years. It all revolves around my extreme skepticism of Jesus and Christianity. I just couldn't understand how people could believe all of that stuff. It bothered me that I didn't have a good reason to believe, but I didn't have a good reason not to. I couldn't shake this feeling of responsibility to understand what I thought about God. *Where do I stand on all of this?* Whether I ended up believing or not, I needed to know *why*. I've spent many years looking into it.

The advantage I think I have, and the reason I think this book is even necessary, is actually because of my inexperience with writing as well as the inexperience with what I'm writing about. The words won't be fluffed because I don't know how to fluff them. My thought process shouldn't go over your head because I haven't been trained to think about this. I'm just a plain and average person trying to navigate through all of my questions about Christianity, God, Jesus, and faith. I don't have it all figured out. I do, though, understand what types of conversations and stories would have helped me in the early stages of trying to understand how people could possibly believe in Jesus and the Bible.

What I hope to do in this book is lead you through my journey from skepticism to faith. I think stories are the easiest way to get into someone's head, so I want to share some of my most personal stories with you. I hope there's one you can relate to that makes you think, *Wait a minute! That's where I find myself right now!*

I don't want this book to sound like I'm telling you what to think and writing *to* you. I want to be exploring all of this *with* you. I want to walk you through the questions I had, and still have, and how I got to the point I find myself at now—writing a book about faith.

I want to take you down my road of struggle, doubt, fear, falling apart, putting myself back together, falling apart again, and finally finding a path that worked for me. I want to motivate you to explore your thoughts on Christianity. I want your life to change in a positive way. I'm like an annoying personal trainer to get you from the couch to a 5K, and maybe even to a marathon someday. Even if—especially if—you don't want to.

I really hope this book speaks to you, motivates you, and gives you practical steps to help your life before and life after look dramatically different. I'm the trainer you never wanted (unless you've been looking for help with some of your deepest questions about faith, which I doubt).

No matter how you feel about me, or God, or faith at the end of this book, I want you to know that doubts and questions are normal and worth looking into. My hope and prayer is that this book makes you think. I want you to actually have a thought out answer when people ask what your thoughts are on Jesus and Christianity.

The Bible says, "And if someone asks about your hope as a believer, always be ready to explain it" (1 Peter 3:15 NLT). After years of reading, now writing, and life happening, I'm now a firm believer in Jesus. I know that some of my friends and family wonder how I got this way. This book is my explanation for the hope that I have.

CHAPTER 1

SMOKING GROUP

Human history is the long terrible story of man trying to find something other than God which will make him happy.

—*C. S. Lewis*

I was sitting in the cafeteria during some of the worst years of my life: junior high. I can still smell the old lunch boxes, hear all the voices echoing off the hard floor, and feel the pit in my stomach as I weave slowly around the tables, hoping certain groups of people make eye contact to show it's okay to sit with them. On this day, I ended up sitting with the cool group, just like I hoped for every day at lunch. Only today would turn out to be a day I wished I'd sat anywhere else. These girls were going around snapping each other's bras and laughing. As much as I wanted to be part of what the cool group was doing, I was hoping I wasn't going to be included because—*oh, great!*—I didn't have a bra yet. I sat there in a cold sweat. I kept my eyes down, hoping they wouldn't try it on me. Why didn't my mom know that most girls my age would need a bra by now? Why did I have to be the oldest kid in my family and have my parents make all these mistakes with me?

My little sister was two years younger than me. She probably already had a bra and would never have to go through the left-out-and-nervous feelings that I was dealing with in the lunchroom that

1

day. I have great parents who would do anything for me, but Ashley was obviously their favorite. At least that's how I felt. She always ended up doing things at the same time or before me, like getting our ears pierced together and having a midnight curfew when I was a senior and she was only a sophomore. She was more of a leader than I was, and everyone said she seemed like the older sister. Plus, she was good at basketball.

In our school, if you were on the traveling basketball team, you were part of the cool group. All I wanted was to be a part of that group. Unfortunately for me, the last basketball game I'd played had been a few years earlier when the only basket I'd scored was on the other team's hoop. I remember dribbling down the court while thinking I must be so fast because nobody was even close to catching me. I shot the ball, and miraculously, it went in. I gave a huge fist pump in the air and looked over at my dad, who was the coach, expecting him to be so proud. He had his head in his hands. Nobody was cheering. I still didn't realize I had just scored for the other team until someone sat me down and told me. That was when I realized basketball wasn't for me.

So I wasn't part of the cool basketball crowd. Well, from what I could tell, the other cool group seemed to be the smoking group. They met behind a gas station next to the school and smoke. I was a big rule follower, so smoking was out of the question. I thought if I just dressed like the smokers, then people would assume I was in their group and think I was cool. I got some super baggy jeans and a black "No Fear" shirt that had some quote about dying. I even got some flannel boxers that I pulled a little above the button of my jeans so people would see them when we had to change for gym class. I got some black velvet Vans shoes. Boom. I was a cool smoker.

Maybe all of this would give me a place to belong. The problem was I only had the one outfit that made me look like I was in the smoking group. Plus, I never talked to anyone from that group. I wore my outfit once a week on Fridays. *Everyone probably thinks I'm so cool*, I thought. But one Friday, one of the popular, pretty girls from the grade above me said I was an "alternative wannabe." I was so embarrassed that she realized I was a faker. I guess it was obvious I wasn't in the smoking group. I didn't wear the outfit again.

At some point, I did get a bra, but that was after people tried snapping mine and made fun of me for not having one. I got my books dumped in the hallway, and some boys made up a rhyme about my chest being as flat as my back. I hated my life in junior high.

There was a group of girls who were nice to me, and I should have hung out with them, but they weren't in the basketball or smoking groups, so they weren't cool enough for me. At the time, I'd rather have had no friends than unpopular friends.

High school got a little better. I was a cheerleader, so at least it looked like I had close friends. I hated cheerleading but thought it was what popular girls did. It was like when I'd tried to look like a smoker, only now I was a cheerleader. At least I really was a cheerleader on the squad. I didn't like it, though, and it was obvious. I felt uncomfortable having the crowd look at me. It felt so fake. I didn't even know if we were on offense or defense.

Why am I doing this? Do the other cheerleaders hate this too? Why am I so awkward?

My mom told me I was the least smiley cheerleader out there. Hopefully, she was the only one who noticed.

I realized the cool kids were going to parties and drinking at houses when parents weren't home. There was one house in particular where the parents were gone every weekend. My natural inclination was to follow the rules, so I didn't want to drink.

Maybe if I just go to the party, people won't realize I'm not drinking and will think I'm part of this group, I thought.

Soon after I started going to the parties, I started drinking. After all, I was a good kid from a good family. I got good grades. I was finally being accepted into a group that I thought was cool. Boys were noticing me. And actually, after a few drinks, I didn't feel so insecure. I loved it. I lived for weekend parties.

Sadly, this would be the pattern for the next ten years. Work hard, party hard, be accepted, be noticed, and belong.

After high school graduation, I went to cosmetology school a few hours away from home. It was right by the college campus, so there were more parties! I'm not sure how I survived the next few years, and now I cringe at some of the dumb things I did. I managed to go to cosmetology school, get jobs at some nice hair salons, move closer to the city, make decent money, have a savings account, and have a good work ethic. I did a lot of dumb things too, like drinking most nights, working on only a few hours of sleep, using a fake ID until I was old enough to drink, sleeping around, taking morning-after pills, blacking out, and getting a DWI.

In the quiet moments, I felt terrible about all these things, but the people I was hanging out with were all doing this too, so I thought it was normal. After all, this was part of growing up.

At least, I'm not older and doing this, I thought. *Isn't this what your late teens and early twenties are meant for? As long as I'm working hard and paying my bills, and I consider myself a nice person from a nice family, it's all good. I'm not hurting anyone. There are people out there doing much worse than this.*

My motivation for all of the partying during that time was attention from guys. That's what I thought I needed to fill the void that had always been in my heart. I was sure the void was there because I never had a core social group. If I could just get a great boyfriend (or any guy to notice me), then I could have him and his group of friends. I was sure that would make me feel complete.

If we were out and a guy chose me over other girls, I felt as if I'd won. He'd picked me over every other girl in the bar. In order to win, I had to look good. I was obsessed with working out, and I didn't miss a day. If I missed a day, I feared that it would become a habit and I would stop looking good. Then I would stop getting attention. Then what would I have? Nothing. So I needed to stay in shape.

I worked out if I was sick or hungover; I'd even work out on holidays. If I could control how I looked, I felt better about my life.

4

I put a lot of pressure on myself to look just right. If the scale said something I didn't like, or if my stomach didn't look as flat as I thought it should, it ruined my day. I never reached my goal weight during that time, but I thought that if I did, then everything in my life would be perfect.

I met guys at parties. I wasn't sure of their goals in life. I only cared if they were cute or funny. I had some long-term boyfriends, and some that didn't last long, but when I was with them, I felt a little better about myself. There were a couple of guys I thought I was in love with and going to marry.

Love is the best feeling. It's so fun getting butterflies when I see my boyfriend. I'm sure our goals and visions for the future will just naturally merge together because of our love. Why would I wreck everything by being the annoying girl who wants to have serious conversations about the direction of life? I'm the fun girl who goes along with whatever.

My self-worth was rooted in other people's acceptance of me. If you had asked me my thoughts on God at this time in my life, I'd probably have rolled my eyes at you before you'd finished your question. I didn't really think about God. I thought I was a good person from a good family and would probably go to heaven if there actually was a heaven. To me, Bible stories were probably made up, but if they were helpful for some people, good for them.

How could anyone possibly know what happened to them when they died anyway? And why would anyone care so much? Get in the real world.

CHAPTER 2

"BOSSBABE"

Pride is a spiritual cancer: it eats up the very possibility
of love or contentment, or even common sense.

—C. S. Lewis

Salon owner—that sounded good. It meant you were smart and worked hard. Self-motivated. Had grit. Independent. "Bossbabe." Yes, sign me up.

I wanted to be seen as a leader. I wanted to do something that people could look up to. Owning a salon seemed like the perfect thing for me. I didn't like the salon I was working at. I could see things that I'd do differently. I'd take my ideas and combine them with what I already knew from the places I'd worked at over the years to create a new salon that I could run exactly how I wanted. I had a feeling other stylists I was friends with would be interested in a new salon like this. I talked about my idea with a few friends, and they said they'd be on board.

I laid awake at night planning it out. I had no idea how to really make it happen, but nothing gave me a bigger rush than figuring out how to make this salon work.

Thankfully, my partying days had slowed down a bit, especially since I'd finally met "the one." I still consider it a miracle that I got someone like my husband. I was out at a bar with my friend, and she spotted him from across the room. She pointed him out to me and said he looked like my type.

I got him to buy me a drink, and then right away, we got into a fight about something. He told me to have a nice life and went back to be with his friends. That's just what I needed in order for me to feel like I was in love—a challenge. Somehow I got him to talk to me again, and I got his number. We dated for a year and a half, and then he proposed.

He had me come over to his downtown condo. He said we were going to go out for dinner. He said he wanted to have a drink before we went out, and asked me to grab what was in the fridge. I opened the fridge to see a bottle of Dom Perignon champagne. It was engraved with the words "I love you! Will you marry me?" I turned around, and he was on one knee with a ring. I said yes. I was so happy! We went out for dinner, and I couldn't get the smile off my face.

I've since asked how he ever decided to marry me, since he takes forever to make decisions and I was such a disaster when I met him. He says it's because he realized he was getting older and all of the good girls were already taken. He said I was the best one he had found in a while, and he figured I was as good as it was going to get. He's so romantic.

He was good looking, calm, and smart. He had a great job. He had it together. He thought I was funny. He gave me confidence, so much confidence that while we were still dating, I told him of my plan to open my own hair salon. He actually thought I should do it.

I was twenty-four years old with no experience in owning a business. I'd gone to nine months of hair school and had worked in a few different salons over the past five years, but that was it. I didn't have any money besides what I made doing hair, and that only covered my townhome mortgage, car payment, and home bills. For some reason, that didn't stop me. I was going to figure out how to make this work. After all, I was a hard worker, and I had grit.

I figured my first step was finding a location for the salon. I found the perfect spot just a few doors down from a Starbucks, and met with the realtor for the strip mall. He asked for my business plan, and I had to admit that I didn't know what that even was.

How embarrassing. It's so obvious I have no clue what I'm doing.

I'm sure he figured this would all be a waste of his time, but he believed me when I told him I'd figure out what a business plan was and have it to him in a few days. I spent the next seventy-two Starbucks-filled hours figuring out what a business plan was and writing one.

Next came the financing part. I had nowhere near enough money to finance this. I did have a group of fourteen stylists who'd agreed to rent chairs at my salon if it ever opened. If I could show that those fourteen stylists could cover all of my projected bills, maybe a bank would help me. I needed a small business loan. I applied for loans and grants through women-in-business types of places and got rejected by all of them. I met with at least ten banks, and was rejected by them. One banker even asked me if I knew that running a business meant more than picking out the paint color for the walls. I smiled, and in my mind, I thanked him for adding fuel to my fire. It was just the motivation I needed to keep going until I figured something out.

Finally, after months of rejection, I found a bank that was willing to give me the loan for the salon. The next six or so months were spent doing hair at two other salons, working on constructing an empty space into a salon, and trying to find stylists willing to work there. I had never been part of the construction of anything, and all of a sudden, I was the one calling the shots on this project. There were nights I sat alone and cried inside the half-built salon because I was scared I'd made mistakes and just wanted to be done with it all. It was too late to back out, though. This was all on my shoulders. My only choice was to make it work.

Onyx Salon opened in May of 2007. I had the fourteen stylists who had committed to working there. It was a risky move on their parts for trusting me. Somehow they had confidence that I knew what I was doing. For the first three years of owning the salon, I was doing hair there, still doing hair at another salon, working at the front desk when I wasn't doing hair, and spending my "day off" at the salon doing odd jobs. There were some days I was there for twenty hours straight only to get up and do it again the next day. It would be six years before I was even able to take home any money from the salon's profit. I only made money from doing hair, but it was okay. I was a hard worker. I was so self-sufficient. I didn't need anyone to help me. Independent. Bossbabe. Busy. Checking things off my list. That's the dream, right?

This will all make me so happy. I'm sure of it.

Somehow within those first three years, besides opening the salon, I also managed to plan our wedding, get married, sell my husband's condo, turn the townhome I owned into a rental property, buy our first home together, open a second salon, and have our first baby. Wow, I was really checking everything off my list! And everything had happened by age twenty-eight, just like I'd planned. I wanted to have one more baby, have it be a girl, and make sure to keep working out every day to keep my figure, and I would have checked everything off my list. I would finally feel content and have a place to belong.

We did go on to do those things. My husband had his successful career as an actuary, and I owned two hair salons. We had a little boy who looked just like my husband, and a baby girl who looked just like me. We owned a beautiful home on the golf course and were drawing up blueprints to put a pool in the backyard.

Set goals and crush them. That's how you earn happiness. We're hard workers and good people from good families. We earned all of this.

My self-worth was rooted in self-sufficiency.

As long as I keep setting goals and checking things off my to-do list, I'll be happy. You've got to earn happiness, and this is how to do it.

If you had asked me my thoughts on God during this time, I would have said (and actually do remember saying), "I think God might be real, but if He is, He's probably so relieved that I'm so self-sufficient. He knows I can take care of myself. He wishes there were more people like me because now He has more time to spend on people who can't help themselves."

What I didn't know then was that I was suffering from *pride*, and it was standing in the way of everything I truly wanted.

Jesus taught that "if you put yourself above others, you will be put down. But if you humble yourself you will be honored" (Luke 14:11 CEV). God knew I needed to be humbled, and He was about to bury me so deep, I had no choice but to do just that.

CHAPTER 3
PERFECT ON PAPER

We are all broken, that's how the light gets in.
—*Ernest Hemmingway*

Our son, Austin, was thirteen months old when I got pregnant with our daughter, Brynn. I had morning sickness with Brynn and a lack of bladder control from Austin's delivery. I remember Austin in his high chair eating breakfast when I got the urge to puke. I didn't want to scare him, so I acted as though I was playing peekaboo with him. I "hid" behind the kitchen island. What I was really doing while I was hiding was puking in the garbage. Because of my lack of bladder control, the puking caused me to full-on pee my pants. I always wore baggy sweatpants, so the pee went straight to the floor. What a mess. Sometimes I wouldn't make it to the garbage and had to puke in the sink. My husband asked that I try my best to puke in the garbage or toilet because he thought it was gross that I puked in the kitchen sink. That annoyed me, so that night I puked in his bathroom sink and didn't clean it up.

After Brynn was born, Austin's way of getting attention was to smear yogurt on his face until it got into his eyes. He then started screaming, and I had to put Brynn down to help him. Then she started crying. I couldn't even get myself a cup of coffee without both of them crying hysterically for leaving them alone in the living room. The whole time my K-Cup of coffee was brewing, I loudly sang songs and

11

waved my arms around so they could see where I was. Then there was the time I was potty training Austin, and he pooped on the floor. The dog ate it. At least I didn't have to clean it up.

When I finally got a chance to clean, it didn't last for long. I worked for hours to put stuff away just to turn around and have a giant mess again. I was so distracted with the kids that when Eric got home, I know he wondered what I'd done all day. The house was a mess, just like when he'd left for work. I was still in my pajamas and hadn't had time to shower. I looked just like I had when he'd left for work every morning. It looked as though I hadn't done anything, but I hadn't sat down all day. I couldn't even explain what I had done because I didn't even know. I did know that I hadn't gotten a chance to do anything I had planned to do. The kids needed me constantly.

There was a day where I decided I was really going to get it together. I was going to surprise Eric by having a spotless house, and I was going to have showered and be out of my pajamas when he got home. Big goals. I ended up getting the house cleaned. I showered. He came home as I was giving the kids a bath.

While I was bathing them, he asked, "Is there water running somewhere else too?"

Then it dawned on me. I had plugged up the sink in the laundry room to clean it, and I'd forgotten to shut the water off. By the time he'd noticed, it had been on for almost a half an hour. Water was everywhere. I had flooded the laundry room. Water was seeping down through the floor and dripping from the basement ceiling. We had to clean it up and put fans everywhere to try to dry the wood.

How have I gotten myself to this point? I can't do anything right.

We joked that I'd spent the whole day cleaning the house and all he'd noticed was that I'd flooded it. Sort of funny, sort of sad. I felt like a failure in everything I did.

Eric was working really long hours during this time, and I had dropped my hours at work to just a few days a week. My second salon was failing, and it was costing me more money than I was making.

After two and a half years of trying to make it work, I had to admit that I needed to close it.

How did I let this happen? The people who work here were counting on me to make this work. How am I going to tell them they've lost their jobs?

I remember my son helping me pack up the salon into boxes. Another failure. At least my first salon was still in business, but for how long? Could I count on that income? What if that one closed too?

Closing the second salon freed up time and money so I could be home more. I was home alone with the kids a lot. It was exhausting. Plus, I was trying to manage the one successful salon with the kids on my hips. That was stressful because when I was at home I felt like I should be at work, and when I was at work, I felt like I should be at home.

I remember being on an important phone call with an unreasonable client who was chewing me out and threatening to contact the Better Business Bureau because she thought she'd gotten poor service from a stylist at the salon. I was at home, and the kids were also screaming at me. I had to run outside and shut the door so the client on the other end of the phone didn't know I was at home with hysterical kids. I need to seem professional. They were screaming and banging their fists on the glass door while this lady was screaming at me on the phone.

Another time, the computers stopped working at the salon. I had to go in to fix the computers, but I had to bring the kids with me. I was at work in a stressful situation while my kids were crawling around the busy salon. I couldn't handle it all. I was so desperate for help, but I was trying to be tough. All of these things were on the list to make me happy. I had even hit my goal weight during this time, so what more could I possibly want?

I remember staring out my kitchen window toward a neighbor's house. I was thinking about how happy she probably was. She was definitely not playing puke-and-pee peekaboo. Her husband probably came home every day by five, gave her a kiss, and they talked about the day. I bet she was cooking everyone a healthy meal that the kids actually ate and that they were all at the dinner table laughing and loving life.

Why isn't my house like that? After all, I've checked all of the boxes that tell me we should have the perfect life. I'm a little stressed, but stress means I'm working hard. If I'm not stressed, I run the risk of it all falling apart. I need to hold this together. Who else can I count on to make this all work? Plus, I'm tough. The responsibility of two kids still in diapers, my now twenty-seven-person salon (and, oh yeah, we got a puppy too), would probably cause anxiety for most people, but not for me. I'm above average in what I can handle.

Busyness and stress became like trophies to me. If I was the busiest person I knew and could say yes to everything that everyone wanted from me, then in my mind I'd won the biggest trophy. It meant I was better at managing life than everyone else. Only, the trophy turned out to be a breakdown. I couldn't handle all of this. I was falling apart. A book I would eventually read described my life perfectly.

> *In my blind need to be seen as hyper-capable, ultra-dependable, that girl who can handle anything, I'd built a life I could no longer handle. My to-do list drove me like an unkind taskmaster. And in my most ground-down moments, I looked over at my friend's life and I saw that she was ... playing. Sheesh. Connecting. Please. Resting. Come on. Asking for help. What a baby.*
> —Shauna Neiquist, *Present Over Perfect*

The life I'd created had become too much for me to handle. I felt I needed to talk to someone about it. I didn't really have any close friends, and I didn't want my husband to think I was weak.

Maybe I need to see a counselor? How embarrassing. I'll make an appointment and never tell anyone about it. I'll have to keep it a secret, or everyone will know I'm losing it. If the girls at the salon know I'm struggling, they'll probably go find another salon to work at where the owner is more stable. I still owe money on my salon loan, and if the stylists leave, I won't be able to pay it off. If I can't pay it off, the bank will take our house. We can't lose our home.

I can't tell Eric. If he knows I'm going crazy, it'll add more stress to his plate. He's pretty stressed at work. I don't want him to have to worry about me too. Plus, I'm the one who wanted to have kids so close in age, and I'm the one who opened the salon, so I'm the one who got myself into this situation.

Why would anyone feel sorry for me? I feel bad wasting anyone's time listening to my self-created sob story, but if I'm paying someone to listen, I won't feel so guilty wasting her time.

I made an appointment to see Missy. I remember sitting in the waiting room and feeling as if I was going to throw up. I looked around.

All of these people probably actually have real problems. What am I even going to tell her? That my life is perfect on paper but I still feel empty?

That was my problem, but what a wuss for needing to see a counselor about it. I wasn't abused, and I hadn't experienced any sort of trauma like the types of people I thought typically saw a counselor. I thought about running out and skipping my appointment, but as I contemplated bolting, she came down and called my name.

Most of what I remember of that first appointment was me crying and telling her I didn't even know why I was really there. My life was perfect, and I had no real problems. Eventually, we got to a point where she explained that I put all of this pressure on myself to hold my perfection on my shoulders and not drop it. I had anxiety about everything in my life. I was trying to relieve the anxiety by trying to control everything.

I had seriously never thought of myself as controlling.

How could I have missed that? I guess I'm trying to control a lot of things, and all it does is make me exhausted. If I'm not in control of my life, then who is?

CHAPTER 4
OUT OF CONTROL

You don't understand now what I'm doing, but someday you will.

—*John 13:7 (NLT)*

I remember my first big experience in not being able to control something. Eric and I had decided to go for it and have a third baby. It was around the time I'd started seeing my counselor but before I truly realized how out of control my life was. I had always envisioned two kids, but maybe it would be fun and spontaneous to add a third. After all, I could probably handle a little more stress.

Since I'd gotten pregnant with the other two pretty easily, we planned what month we would get pregnant so we'd know what month the baby would be born.

I eat right, work out, take care of my body, and am a good person, so this pregnancy will go as smoothly as the other two.

Of course, I got pregnant just as planned. I could feel a slight cramping, which told me my body was working on making this baby. I remember thinking the cramping felt stronger than I remembered in the past. That probably meant this pregnancy was really strong and my body was doing the right thing.

I was about seven weeks along and loving that we had this special secret. Eric and I were getting ready for a friend's wedding, and I was planning out how I would have to get water with a lime in it so people

16

wouldn't realize I wasn't drinking. The kids were at my husband's parents since we'd planned on staying the night at the hotel. I was doing my nails by the pool before getting into the shower. Eric and I were talking about baby names and how we were so crazy for having a third.

I went inside to go to the bathroom before my shower, and I saw blood. A lot. I knew right away what that meant. Miscarriage. Deep down, I think I knew the cramping wasn't necessarily a good sign, but I'd chosen to ignore it. Until now. I called Eric inside and sobbed.

Since I was so tough, I decided we could still go to the wedding. I'd suck it up. I stopped crying and got ready. We went to the wedding and reception. I remember feeling so sad about the miscarriage.

How could this be happening? Things like this don't happen to me.

As soon as I started feeling like crying during the wedding, I shoved it back inside. I didn't want to seem like a wimp. I toughed it out. I remember ordering wine at the reception and feeling so sad that I was now able to drink it. I hardly sipped it because what if somehow there was a chance this wasn't a miscarriage? I knew it was, though.

I tried to laugh at everyone's jokes, and pay attention to what was going on in their lives. At one point, one of the guys at the table even proposed a toast to "none of the girls at the table being pregnant so we can all drink together tonight!" Seriously. I smiled, toasted, and sipped my wine.

This was my first of three total miscarriages in trying for our third baby. I eventually went to an infertility clinic. They took lots of blood and did ultrasounds and other tests. After months of appointments, I found out I had a blood-clotting problem. I was sent to a hematologist, and was told that I actually have two genetic mutations that caused my blood to clot too fast. There was no doubt that this was causing the miscarriages.

I asked how it was possible that I'd had my first two kids without complications, and the doctor said, "Luck." Only 20 percent of pregnancies would go to full term with someone who had what I had. Many mothers don't find out they have it until their baby is stillborn.

What? Of all the things I worried about and tried to control during my pregnancies, this was never something that had crossed my mind. How did I have my two kids without complications?

She told me my next pregnancy could be helped if I give myself blood thinner shots right when I find out I was pregnant again, but eventually we decided that two kids was enough. It was the first time I gave up on something that I really wanted and thought I should be able to control. For a long time, I felt like I was leaving behind a person that I envisioned having. Like I was giving up on this little baby we thought we would have. I picture myself walking out on a baby that we had already named. It was hard to move on. I don't know why we didn't get to have that third baby. Was there some sort of plan for my family that I wasn't in control of?

Shortly before the miscarriages, we decided we should probably find a church to go to.

For the kids, not me.

Growing up, my family usually went on Christmas and sometimes Easter.

We were really good people, so we didn't really need church. Plus, weekends were for sleeping in.

My family was Lutheran, and I had gotten baptized as a baby and confirmed in junior high, but I didn't really know why or what any of it really meant. I was too busy trying to be cool and act as if it was all a waste of time. I always did feel good when we would went to church, like it was something wholesome people did. It was nice to check "do a good thing" off my list.

Eric and I tried out a few churches and found one that we thought was fine. It felt how I expected it to. Uncomfortable and boring, but wholesome. The people there were overly excited to see a new family. It made me want to hide.

Why are we doing this?

In my mind, all of the women were running around, worried if there would be enough coffee and napkins for everyone.

How annoying. They probably didn't even know what real stress was.

They were probably thinking about how much better they were than everyone else. I'm sure they are planning potlucks where churchy women could get together and judge everyone else.

I knew people who were much nicer than them who didn't even go to church. But good for them, I guess. If that's what you need to make you happy. I'm not here to judge.

One day, a client at the salon was telling me they'd found a really good church that I should check out. I didn't love the one we were at, and this client was someone I looked up to. We decided to go to this new church for the Christmas Eve service that year.

I remember picking out cute outfits for our little kids. After all, that was the whole point of this—to have the cutest family in the best outfits and to look adorable at church. Brynn had on this red-lace dress with sequins. I think she was starting to come down with croup, but I didn't have time to think about that. We went anyway. We did look cute, and I bet nobody could tell that Bynn was sick and I was a wreck.

We checked the kids into their area. Eric and I found a spot way in the back of the church. I didn't want anyone to talk to us and realize we were a new family. I had learned that lesson from the last church we had been at. We wanted to stay in the back, in the dark, and be left alone.

The music was fine, and then it was time for the message. I wasn't expecting it to be anything special, but something happened to me at that Christmas service. I actually loved it. It made sense. I was drawn in. I even thought about it throughout the week. I wanted to hear more. Eric and I decided that this would be our new church.

We started going fairly regularly. *For the kids.* I remember that whenever I felt drawn into the message, I tried and snap myself out of it.

I need to keep my guard up and my walls up. I don't want to get brainwashed by all of this and turn into an obnoxious church person who talks about God everywhere she goes. After all, I have it all together and am self-sufficient. I don't need church or anything else.

All of these people who love it here are probably just desperate for something to help them with life. I wonder if they have even stopped to realize that none of this even makes sense? I wish I was as naive as them to just blindly believe all of this. They've probably never even questioned any of this. Lucky them for not having to think things through. If they did, they would never be able to have any proof that any of this is true. I won't ask, though. I don't want to burst their bubble. I guess I've been cursed with common sense.

We kept going, and I tried to keep my walls up. I had other friends who had gotten really wrapped up in this whole Jesus thing, and I didn't want to become like that. Besides, anytime I asked them anything about Christianity or why they believed, they just recited a Bible verse.

Maybe that seemed like a good answer to them, but to someone like me who wasn't even sure if I believed in the Bible, a Bible verse was meaningless.

Just have faith was another answer I got. How is that an answer? Every religion has faith in what they believe. How is having faith in Jesus any different from having faith in Allah, or nature, or good vibes, or juju, or faith in karma, or good things happening to good people? People have faith in what their horoscope says and what psychics say. Everyone has faith in something, even if it's just faith in themselves.

It's not that I have a problem with faith in general, but I'm not just going to put my faith into something because it sounds nice or because it doesn't offend anybody. I need to put my faith in something that is real, that can be trusted, and that can be proven.

I had questions about science, historical facts, why Jesus, and more. I didn't hear anyone else asking questions like this, so I just figured nobody had the guts to actually look into this stuff for fear that they wouldn't come up with any answers and their whole belief system would crumble.

I couldn't help but wonder, though. Were my miscarriages part of God's plan for my life? Was God calling the shots in my life? I didn't really have an answer for why some things weren't going according to my plans.

Another thing I had to admit was everything that I thought would make me happy didn't last very long. I was always looking for the next thing. I thought that when I reached my goal weight, I'd be happy. If I had that outfit, that car, that house, got married, had kids, had clearer skin, if my arms were more toned, I had more friends, more money, less taxes, a different president—you name it, I thought it. The fact is, none of that would satisfy me.

I read something about rich people and celebrities being the most depressed because they could buy anything and go anywhere they wanted. People loved them, and they had adoring fans everywhere they went. For most of us, we assumed we would have happiness if only we had those things. They say rich and famous people are the most depressed because they actually have those things, and realize they still have an emptiness. I'm not rich or famous, but I could totally relate.

What does it take, then, to feel fulfilled? There has to be more to life than this.

I didn't know at the time (and probably wouldn't have cared), but there was a man in the Bible named Solomon. He was the richest and wisest man who had ever lived at that time. He was on a quest to find what could satisfy him in life. He had many wives, homes, servants, and anything else he saw. He had as much knowledge and power as he could have ever wanted. In the end, his conclusion was that nothing on earth could make him happy. It was all a meaningless quest, like chasing the wind. It's like we're all chasing something, and when we catch it, it doesn't satisfy us.

If all of this stuff is meaningless, what am I doing all of this for? What's anyone doing here? What's the point of life?

CHAPTER 5
GOTTA HAVE FAITH

Blind faith, no matter how passionately expressed, will not suffice.

—E. O. Wilson

"I've just always believed" is one of the most frustrating comments I hear. I've even heard people say it with a braggy tone, as though they're more special because they never had doubts. One woman told me she'd been baptized at age seven and never looked back.

Really? You've never thought this all sounded a little unrealistic? You're saying at age seven you knew everything you needed to know in order to understand why you're choosing to follow God? You're certain the one God you happened to get taught about at age seven is, ironically, the only one of all the gods that's the correct one? You've never thought you should look into it to confirm that belief?

Another woman said she'd read through the Bible twice and just couldn't get herself to believe. Although I ultimately disagreed with her decision to not believe, I had more respect for her decision since she had at least put effort into knowing why she didn't believe.

I'm so happy that right now my kids believe what I do. At the level in which they can think and reason, they have chosen to believe in God. That makes my heart happy. I sure hope someday, though, they reexamine their beliefs. I don't want them to believe just because I told them to back when they were little. I hope what I have taught them, and my influence, has a big impact on their decisions, but it shouldn't be the only reason for their beliefs.

There's power in knowing *why* you believe in something. There's a confidence in having solid reasons to believe that can relieve anxiety and doubt. I wonder if, at the core of fear of the future and anxiety for *believers*, is a sliver of doubt, whether you want to admit it or not? If you truly, fully, wholeheartedly believe in God, without a doubt, you shouldn't worry about the future. God tells believers that we don't have to worry. We all do to some degree, though. If we can close the "unbelief gap," I think we could live better lives with less fear of the future because we could fully trust that our lives are in God's hands.

How do we know what to believe in? If I'm going to make all of my life decisions based on some sort of standard, I need to know what I'm choosing and why. I need to look into different possibilities of what to have faith in, and then choose the one that makes the most sense.

My first step was figuring out how I thought the world began. Was it by chance or by some sort of god? Mark Cahill said, "You may find it hard to believe that God turned nothing into everything. But the alternative is that nothing turned itself into everything."

Nothing turning itself into everything is evolution. What does that theory look like?

What if we've just all evolved into what we've become now? It seems as if people who believe the world happened by chance *instead* of God want to think of themselves as too smart to fall for what's written in the Bible. They aren't gullible or dumb enough to believe all of the stuff in the Bible actually happened. They've had too much education and have studied more than average people, so they're just too superior in intelligence to fall for anything that can't be proven. It's almost fun for them to see all of those dumber, uneducated people try to figure out how the world began.

Evolution says there was a big bang that formed an ocean on earth. Then out of the ocean came two nonliving particles called amino acids. The two amino acids came together and eventually, somehow, turned into a single living cell. Over time, that cell turned into fish, birds, animals, and humans. So, two nonliving particles somehow turned into living things and, over time, turned into humans.

Evolution says that, given enough time, two nonliving things can turn into people. *Does that make sense? Not really.* Nobody can prove this. It takes a leap of faith to go with it.

Scientists say that life has to come from life. Something can't come from nothing. Evolution says something *did* come from nothing, just because enough time had passed.

Think about your car. Did someone design it, or did random parts just happen to come together to make your car? Because there's a car, there must be a car maker. What about people? Because there are people, there has to be a "people maker." When you look at the universe, earth, and everything on it, do you think it points to a maker, or a random chance of cells coming together?

The probability of evolution being true is the same probability of a tornado sweeping through a junkyard and forming at the other end a Boeing 747.
—Sir Fred Hoyle

If we've all just evolved, why do we have emotions such as sadness, excitement, joy, sympathy, anticipation, or love? Why do we have a sense of right and wrong? Why do we feel good when we have senses of purpose? Why do we get good feelings by helping others? How do we know that hurting a child is just wrong? Why do we all have the desire to be loved? Evolution can't answer that.

Scientists say there are seventy-five finely tuned aspects to the world, and if any one is a bit off, life would not be possible. If the earth was one degree closer to the sun, we would burn up. If it was one degree further, we'd freeze. If gravity was any weaker, oceans would empty into space. If the mix of nitrogen and oxygen in the air was one part stronger or one part weaker, we couldn't breathe. Scientists say there are seventy-five of these finely tuned aspects going on for life to exist.

Science can explain the *how*—God explains the *why*.

Sir Isaac Newton wrote more papers about God than he did about science. I didn't realize that. I assumed that since he was a scientist, he didn't believe in God. He said, "Gravity explains the motions of the planets, but it cannot explain who set the planets in motion. God designs along rational and universal principles."

Louis Pasteur, the founder of microbiology and immunology, said, "Little science takes you away from God but more of it takes you to Him."

If you trust science, you can also trust God. I think of science as labels for everything God has made. It's like a scavenger hunt to keep us busy trying to figure out the world. Sometimes I picture God looking down at scientists and watching how excited they are about cracking the codes and figuring out how He made the world.

At this point, it will take a bigger leap of faith for me not to believe in a creator, a god, but which god do I believe in?

Comedian Ricky Gervais sarcastically summed up what I had been thinking, "There have been nearly 3000 Gods so far but only yours actually exists. The others are silly made up nonsense. But not yours. Yours is real."

Sad, but true. Just because I grew up in a home and country in which the God of Christianity is the most popular, that means that the first and only God I've learned about happens to be the right one? How fair is that to other people who grew up believing something else? How arrogant to think that I know which one is real and they don't.

I need to look into other gods and why people would believe in them. What makes the God of Christianity so much more real than other gods? Don't all roads lead to God?

What if only one road leads to God? I need to figure out what that road is.

The thing that seemed the fairest was just to believe that all roads lead to God. We can never know which one is true, so let's just all be good people and assume that is good enough. This is actually a common thing to do in our culture right now. People aren't interested in picking one god. They take a little bit of what they know about different gods and religions, and sort of have a mix of whatever feels right to them. That way you don't have to commit to anything.

There are many reasons people feel like this. People question what the church is teaching, some don't like churches' positions on social and political issues, and some consider religion irrelevant to their life.

I have felt every one of those things and more, but I just couldn't be satisfied with that answer. Something has to be right, and everything else has to be wrong. Everything can't be right (or wrong), and it can't be based on whatever you feel at any given time. I need more proof than just thinking "everything works" (or nothing works).

Ravi Zacharias says, "Truth cannot be sacrificed on the altar of tolerance. Some beliefs are false, and we know them to be false. To deem all religions equally true is sheer nonsense for the simple reason that they contradict each other." (If you would like to learn more about Christianity in comparison to other religions, go to YouTube and look up Ravi Zacharias. He's great to listen to and has a cool accent.)

For a long time, I felt there wasn't enough evidence to prove any religion right or wrong. Had I ever looked into any evidence for any religion? No, but I assumed there wasn't any. Did I know anything about any other religions to try to understand if they seemed logical? No. I just assumed nothing was any different nor had more proof than anything else. Should I look into these things if I'm going to try to make an informed decision? *Yes.*

Well, this sounds boring.

It was kind of boring, but also very interesting. I read a lot and listened to podcasts about different gods and why people believe in them. I didn't look into every possible god, but I did look at the major religions. I'll give you a brief overview of the top three so you can get an idea of how different they all are. My main goal of looking at these was trying to answer the question, "What's the proof?"

26

Hinduism is one of the world's largest religions. According to Hinduism, anything can be a god. Trees, cars, bugs, or animals can be gods. Hinduism has over 330 million potential gods. They believe if you obtain a high enough level of consciousness, you too can become a god. You could be one, and so could your friend. Hinduism says we're all gods in the making—we just need to realize it.

Your only hope is to do enough good in the world so when you're born again as something else, it's at a higher level than what you're currently at. They believe in reincarnation, which is continuing to be born as different things. You keep being born as different things, and you were possibly thousands of different bodies before you became human. You might come as a lower creature next, but your hope is that someday you can stop the cycle of being born as different things, and be separated from having a body at all, which is a state of "nothingness." You can earn this state by a number of things, such as keeping vows, giving alms to gods, and sometimes self-torture. There's no heaven. You just hope you don't come back as a lower form, such as an insect.

The belief is that the doer of good becomes good; the doer of evil becomes evil. We call it karma. Seems fair, I guess. From what I could understand, their "proof" is an individual experience. If you can't find it, you're not focused enough on your inner self.

Where is the evidence for this? I couldn't find any.

Islam is another large religion. Muslims believe in one god. Many believe it's actually the same God as Christianity. The difference is, in Islam, they don't believe God wants a relationship with you, and they don't believe He loves you, forgives you, or is interested in your life.

They believe Jesus was a prophet (a teacher of God), but not the son of God. They call their god Allah. They believe Muhammad was the final prophet of God. Muhammad's visions were used to write their bible, called the Quran.

In Islam, you have to *earn* God's favor. You're not forgiven for sins just by being Muslim. You need to work your way to heaven. You have to keep trying really hard, but you're never sure if it's good enough. It's a constant state of striving. You're constantly trying to keep all of the rules, and if you don't, they believe you're punished. The way to earn heaven is by reciting the creed (that Allah is god and Muhammad is the messenger), praying five times per day (after washing your body in a certain way), giving alms, fasting for thirty days a year (on Ramadan), and making a pilgrimage to Mecca (visiting this holy city). You're saved by your own human effort. You hope it's good enough.

The religion hinges on Muhammad's visions. He was a prophet who lived over six hundred years after Jesus's time. His first revelations were while alone in the woods. He claims God appeared to him in a cave and then gave him visions for the next twenty or so years. Nobody else had these visions. They rely on Muhammad's claims. Is that enough proof? Visions that couldn't be proven? Not for me.

Christianity says there's only one God. He invites everyone into a personal relationship with Himself. God is superior to all and isn't limited to a body. He is everywhere, and He comes in the form of the Father, Son (Jesus), and Holy Spirit. He gives love, joy and peace. He is personal and loving. He brought his son to earth, as Jesus. Jesus is God in human form.

We've been separated from God because of sin. We've all sinned and fallen short of God's standard. The penalty for sin is death. There's a way to escape eternal death and go to heaven. You don't have to earn it. It's a free gift. You get to heaven by believing in Jesus and accepting God. That's it.

What's the proof for this? Jesus is the proof. We'll look into Jesus and his story in the next chapter.

These religions all claim different things. There goes my theory of "all religions are pretty much the same and all roads lead to God." If one of these religions is true, the others have to be false because they're all so different from each other.

Every other religion says you need to *do* something to be saved. Christianity is the only one that says you don't have to do anything. It's done by Jesus. He has paid the price for us, and all we have to do is receive the free gift of eternal life.

This led me to my next logical question. Who is Jesus? What's Jesus's story, and what's the proof? Why did so many people want to write about Jesus? Did Jesus really die and then come back to life?

I agree with Pastor Andy Stanley, who said, "When somebody predicts their own death and resurrection and pulls it off, we should go with whatever that person says."

Did Jesus really do that?

CHAPTER 6

CHOCOLATE BUNNIES

It is possible to become a Christian because of the evidence rather than in spite of the evidence.

—J. Warner Wallace

If Jesus actually died on the cross and then came back to life three days later, that's the proof I need in order to let my guard down and allow the messages at church to start sinking in. Could that really be true?

Is this all just a giant waste of time? I wanted to soften my heart, but couldn't do it without evidence. *Is any of this true, or is it just nice words and wishful thinking?* I kept hearing my pastor talk about a relationship with Jesus. *What in the world does that mean? How would you even do that? Have a relationship with someone who is invisible? Sounds like a crazy cult.*

Easter. Candy and chocolate bunnies. That's what I thought of when I would think about Easter. Dyeing eggs with the kids sounded fun until we actually tried it. There was a mess everywhere, and the kids always fought over the colors. There was glitter everywhere. The picture I posted on Facebook always made it look fun, though. We make Easter nests out of chow mein noodles and butterscotch chips with M&M's in the middle as the eggs. The Kids have an Easter egg hunt with their cousins and get prizes. That was the point of Easter, right? To have brunch, look for eggs, and try to get the kids to take a pic with a weird-looking bunny?

Growing up, we sometimes went to church on Easter and sang songs saying, "Jesus is alive" (whatever that meant). I didn't put much thought into it or really know why people were singing that.

Turns out, all of Christianity is based on this event. Easter is about Jesus dying and then coming back to life three days later. If this really happened, it would be some pretty significant proof that Jesus is the Son of God, just like he said he was. Then we could trust everything he said. Did it really happen?

Almost all historians agree that Jesus was an actual person in history, but they don't agree upon whether or not he was the Son of God. Most of the information about Jesus came from the written accounts of Jesus's life that eventually turned into the Bible.

If you're wondering, *How do I know if I can trust the Bible?* then we're on the same page. This part was a stumbling block for me. It took me a long time to look into and ultimately trust. I spent years digging into facts to prove whether or not the Bible is reliable and if Jesus is the Son of God. It's one of my favorite things to read about. The more proof I find, the closer I feel to God.

Unfortunately, the feedback I've gotten is that this topic is very boring and uninteresting to most people. I want to write pages and pages about it, but you'll quit reading this book because it will probably bore you. If you're completely satisfied in the fact that Jesus actually *is* the Son of God, then you can skip this chapter. It's fine. You can get right back into chapter 7 without missing anything.

If you aren't convinced that Jesus is the Son of God, here are a couple of things to think about, and then we can move on.

There has been no archeological discovery made that can contradict what the Bible says. It's the most accurate ancient writing in history. Josh McDowell, after searching for evidence for Christianity, said, "I found evidence. Evidence in abundance. I had to admit that the Old and New Testament documents were some of the most reliable writings in all antiquity."

If the reliability of the Bible is something that you question, I would suggest doing these two things: read or watch the movie *The*

Case for Christ by Lee Strobel, and listen to the four-part series called "The Bible for Grown-Ups" by Andy Stanley on YouTube. These were the most impactful and easiest to understand. I read way more about it in other books, but these were my favorite.

Stanley said, "The stunning thing about the Bible is *not* that God wrote it. What's stunning? The texts that make up the Bible were written by over forty men over a period of about 1,500 years, and yet they tell one story. That's amazing."

That actually is amazing. It's like a giant timeline. The beginning is when God created the world. The "middle" is when Jesus came. We haven't gotten to the end yet. According to Christianity, you and I are in this story. We're somewhere in between the middle and end.

The Bible even tells us the ending. Jesus comes back again, and those who believe will live with Him in heaven. We don't know when, but we can count on it happening.

Why would people write about Jesus? When Jesus was around, there was no "Christian Bible." There wasn't any such thing yet. What did Jesus do that was so significant that they would have to make a whole book and religion about him? If you guessed "dying and coming back to life," you're right. #congrats

So, Jesus was going around telling everyone that he is the Son of God. Pretty weird. Today, if someone were to tell you that, you would say they were crazy, probably mentally ill. We know Jesus wasn't mentally ill because his teachings made so much sense. He was consistent. When psychologists and psychiatrists from today evaluate Jesus, they find no evidence that he was mentally ill.

Fine. He wasn't mentally ill. Maybe he was just a nice person and a wise teacher. That sounds more realistic. Many people are comfortable saying he was an important and wise teacher, just not the Son of God. Think about this: Would a nice person tell everyone to abandon the lives they were living to follow him, if he knew he really wasn't God's son? If he convinced everyone that he was God's son, and said if they follow him they would go to heaven, but he knew that wasn't really true, that would make him a liar. Was He a liar? If you're willing to admit He was a good person, you're contradicting yourself, because good people aren't liars.

If He was a liar, then how did He pull this next thing off? He died and came back to life. How do we know that? One piece of evidence is that people won't let themselves be killed over something they know was a lie. Who would die for a lie?

As Jesus was dying on the cross, people were mocking Him. They were telling Him that if He was really God's son, He should be able to save Himself. His followers were watching this person they loved and believed in die, seemingly unable to save Himself.

The rulers at that time were happy. Finally, Jesus was out of the way. His followers were proven wrong. Their "king" was dead. If He was really God, He would have saved Himself. Now everything could get back to normal.

Jesus's dead body was taken off the cross and put in a tomb. We know He was dead because the men who were in charge of these executions were trained killers. If they didn't do their jobs, they would be killed themselves. They made sure He was dead before taking Him off the cross.

Jesus's followers wondered how they could have been so wrong about Him. What about all He had taught and said about Himself? He must have lied to them. They went home feeling terrible. They were also scared. They trusted Jesus would protect and save them, but now He was gone. Followers of Jesus got thrown in jail or killed, so many hid for fear of being hurt.

On the third day after Jesus died, some women went to His tomb. They noticed the stone in front of the tomb had been rolled to the side. Jesus's body was gone. An angel appeared and said Jesus wasn't there because He was alive. He came back to life.

The women ran to tell Jesus's closest followers the news. At first, they didn't believe it. They thought there was no way this could be true. Until they actually saw Jesus. He was alive and walking with them. He was talking with them. One man, Thomas, was someone I can totally relate to. He didn't believe it was really Jesus. You may have heard the phrase "doubting Thomas." This is why. It wasn't until Thomas actually touched Jesus's hands and saw the holes in them from being pounded with nails into the cross, that he finally believed.

Over five hundred people saw Jesus alive after His death. They were telling everyone about this crazy thing that happened. I'm sure if YouTube was around at that time, it would have gone viral.

One person Jesus appeared to after His death was His brother, James. Prior to Jesus's death, James didn't believe Jesus was the Son of God. Can you blame him? How would you feel if your brother was making those claims? James watched His brother die on the cross. Then James saw Jesus alive again. Then James believed.

James went on to become the leader of the church in Jerusalem. James would eventually be put to death for his beliefs.

How did James become so sure that his brother was the Son of God? The answer is simple—he saw his brother alive from the dead, as many others did.

The same people who had been scared and hiding after Jesus died now were bravely sharing their faith in Him. The people who had just denied knowing Him three days prior were now on record as being willing to die for believing in Him, and many died torturous deaths because of it.

Why would they do that? What could have possibly changed their minds in those three days so much that they would go from being hopeless and denying Him, to confidently saying they believed in Him, knowing that admitting it would likely get them killed?

Who would die for something they knew was a lie? They had to have seen Him alive after dying on the cross, just as the Bible says.

In the Old Testament of the Bible, there were men called prophets. God gave them information as to what was going to happen in the future. I can hear you thinking that this doesn't make sense, but just go with it for now. Prophets told people about what it would be like in the future, when God brought his Son to earth. God wanted people to be absolutely positive that Jesus was the one to follow. Just as we all have addresses to our homes, these predictions given by the prophets were like Jesus's address. It singled Him out as the one. God didn't want us to miss this.

There were many specific predictions about what it would be like when God's Son came down to us. They were written hundreds of years prior to Jesus being born. Guess who fulfilled 333 of these predictions? Jesus.

Some of these predictions included Jesus's place of birth, time of birth, manner of birth, manner of death, and His burial. These are things that can't be faked.

Maybe this is all coincidence? What are the chances?

Well, Josh McDowell says the chance of just fulfilling eight prophecies goes something like this. Let's say you take the state of Texas, and cover it two feet deep with silver dollars. You take one of those silver dollars and put a red X on it. You take bulldozers and stir it all up. Then you blindfold someone and have them walk through Texas. You randomly have them stop somewhere and pick up a silver dollar. The chances of them grabbing the silver dollar with the red X is the same probability of Jesus fulfilling just *eight* of the predictions. So is it just by chance he fulfilled 333? I don't think so. Jesus is the one.

If you need more proof, please read the book *More Than a Carpenter* by Josh McDowell. I just gave a couple of examples from the book, but there are many more.

One more big issue for me was Christians seemed to have all sorts of rules. It's like this club that says they're welcoming and inviting, but what they really want is for you to follow all of their rules. They make you feel "less than" them, and like they have it all together and you don't.

A friend of mine invited me to her church when I was in my wild phase in my early twenties. Right after the invite, she told me I'd probably burst into flames when I walked through the doors because of all the bad things I had done. What a warm welcome.

Do I have to be perfect to enter a church? Does God only want religious people who have always followed the rules? What about people who are messed up, like me? Am I not welcome? For some reason I still went with her. I don't remember anything about it except the burning-in-flames comment. I never went with her again.

Sadly, she was misrepresenting what it means to be a Christian. I see this on social media all of the time. Someone brings up God, and the whole thread blows up with arguments for and against God. Everyone loses their temper, and everyone looks bad. Almost everyone ends up behaving in the opposite way that Jesus showed us. This is a misrepresentation of what it looks like to follow Jesus. Poorly behaving Christians are a perfect justification for a nonbeliever to keep not believing.

If this is how Christians behave, then no thanks.

A Christian's number one job is to love others. In fact, as Jesus was dying on the cross, the last command he gave was to love one another. It's really that simple.

All of us are sinners. The church should be thought of as more of a hospital. You don't go because you're healthy—you go because you need help. Some sins are more obvious than others, but we all sin and fall short of who God calls us to be. Instead of looking down at one another or feeling less than another person, we should realize that we're all in the same boat of falling short. We all need forgiveness. Nobody is better than anyone else. If someone makes you think God wouldn't accept you because of your sins, then they're misrepresenting Jesus's message.

I'm a hairstylist. I have done hair for the past seventeen years. I love all of my clients. I like to think I have a sense of style and know what would and wouldn't look good on someone. Many clients love to tell others that I do their hair, and I'm glad they do. They're good representations of my hair business, and I'm proud that they tell others about my work.

Then there are other clients who are very specific about what they want me to do to their hair. Some of the time, I don't think it looks good, and it's something I would never do if it were up to me.

One of those clients was telling me how she was trying to get her friend to come and see me for her hair, but couldn't figure out why she wasn't making an appointment. I knew why. It's because this client's hair was terrible. I appreciate that she was telling others about me, but she was misrepresenting me. I didn't want her hair to be the example of my work. I would cringe when I pictured her telling others that I did her hair. Her hair was turning more people away from me than getting them to want to see me.

I wonder if God ever feels like that when some people try to represent Christianity? Are there times when God looks down, wishing certain people wouldn't act as they do in His name? Maybe they're turning more people away from Him by their behavior. They're misrepresenting what it means to be a Christian.

I had to admit to myself that when I wanted to prove that God or Christianity wasn't the right thing to get involved with, I thought of the worst representation of a Christian I could come up with. I thought of someone who claimed to be a Christian but also lied, stole, or judged everyone. Sometimes I thought about a priest who was molesting kids. I used them as my reasons not to associate with Christianity, as if God were the one making them do these terrible things. Why was I blaming Jesus/God/the Bible for people doing things that are the opposite of what Christianity actually teaches?

I needed to base my judgments of Christianity on the teachings of Jesus, not on other poorly behaving Christians.

Fine. My reasons for being a skeptic are invalid. I'm ready to move on.

I wasn't sure what "moving on" meant yet, until I read this quote from Billy Graham. Someone asked him, "Why, if Christianity is so valid, is there so much evil in the world?"

He replied, "With so much soap, why are there so many dirty people in the world? Christianity, like soap, must be personally applied if it's to make a difference in our lives."

Um, okay, so I'm ready to personally apply it. How do I do that? I don't really feel any different. I believe, now what?

37

CHAPTER 7

TINFOIL EYES

To trust God in the light is nothing, but to trust him in the dark - that is faith.

—C. H. Spurgeon

There were five things that our church said were the "next steps" to take once you believe. I started to do some of them, such as volunteering at church and trying to read the Bible. It just felt so fake. I still had my walls up. I wanted the walls to come down, but I didn't know how. It's like I was scared to let my guard down because I felt unsure of what would happen to me if I did.

I would eventually learn that what I needed to do was *submit* to God and His plans for my life. That word scared me. Submitting your life to God isn't easy. Plus, I wasn't sure how to do that.

We had a five-year-old boxer, but this summer I decided we needed to get a bulldog puppy. When I first told my husband about my idea of getting another dog, he said it was one of the worst ideas I'd had. He then reminded me that I'd had a lot of bad ideas. We already had one dog, why would we need another? I took his opinion into consideration. Two weeks later, Daisy was ours.

I love her, but she can get wild. A dog trainer told me that Daisy needed to learn that *I* was in charge, not her. She needed to submit to me. One way to get her to do this was to hold her down on the ground and lay on top of her so she couldn't get up. She squirmed around because she didn't like it, but I needed to keep holding her down until she gave up and submitted to me. She needed to learn that I was in charge, and I got to decide when she was ready to get up. The sooner she submitted and stopped squirming, the sooner I let up on her. This taught her that I was in control.

Life would be better for her once she learned that I was in charge. I was not holding her down because I hated her. It was actually because I loved her and wanted her to let me teach her. She needed to learn the order of things. I was the leader. She was just a puppy, so she needed to learn how to stay safe. If she didn't learn to listen to me, she could run out into the road and get hit by a car. Or she could do what our other dog did and eat a whole loaf of bread and then have projectile diarrhea all over my carpet. The smell was so bad that I had to actually use a razor blade to cut out my carpet in two different places as I was dry heaving. At least we got new carpet in our bedroom. The point is, she was better off when she listened to me instead of doing her own thing.

I was about to see what it was like to submit to God. God was going to take my life into His hands and give me a chance to submit to His plans for it instead of my own plans. This was going to be painful. I didn't realize what was going on at first. I was like a panicked puppy getting held down by my life. I was squirming around and trying to do things my own way. Finally, it became too much. I stopped squirming. I was ready to try things God's way. I submitted.

Growing up, we had a lake cabin we went to on the weekends. We had a creek running through the lot, and we caught frogs and turtles in there. We fished, skied, tubed, swam, and had bonfires. The lake cabin had become my safe spot. Ever since we'd gotten it when I was eight, I'd gone there and all of my problems had disappeared. Even in my twenties, I had gone and felt as though I was a little kid again. When I needed to escape from the world, that's where I'd gone.

When I had kids of my own, I made sure the lake was special to them too. It was so fun watching them enjoy the exact same things that I had as a kid. My plan was to make sure it stayed in our family forever, and it would become my kids' and grandkids' favorite place someday.

One game my sister and I had played there when we'd been young was something we'd called "tinfoil eyes." We'd made it up, and it sounds so dumb now, but we'd thought it was the best game ever. We'd taken tinfoil, put it in our goggles, and used that like a blindfold. The other person had spun you around with the goggles on, and then had led you through the trees, on the dock, and around the creek. If they'd told you to go left, you had gone left. If they'd told you to jump, you had jumped (usually because you were jumping over the creek). If you hadn't listened carefully and trusted their instructions, you had fallen in the water or stepped on something you hadn't wanted to (like the time my sister had "accidently" had me step in dog poop). Then, after a while, you had to guess where you were on the property. If you'd guessed correctly, you had gotten a point. We had played that game for hours.

Submitting was basically learning how to play tinfoil eyes, only with God leading me. God wants us to walk by faith, not by sight. If you can get in tune with how He speaks to you, He will guide you, even though you don't know where He's taking you. You trust that He will always lead you to the place you were meant to be, even if you can't see where you're going. It's called faith. It doesn't sound too hard until you're in a situation that rocks you to the core.

I got rocked to the core. It's how I finally broke down and submitted. I couldn't rely on my own strength to get through these next series of events. Cue Carrie Underwood: "Jesus, take the wheel."

Around the time I was feeling fake while taking my "next steps" at church, we decided to take a family trip to Florida. We were just trying to heal from the three miscarriages that had happened throughout the fall and winter, and we'd thought it would be nice to take our minds off of that. I had convinced Eric that we needed to rent this cute, turquoise house right on the beach. The kids still needed naps and quiet time, so we could just put them in the house while we sat outside on the beach. Perfect!

We had been looking forward to the trip. We got new swimming suits, and cute carry-on suitcases for the kids. We set our alarms for our early morning flight.

Brynn had a little cold, but other than that, the flight went smoothly. We got into our rented a car and Google mapped the address to our vacation house. We pulled up and could feel the warm ocean air on our skin.

We were excited to see that the house was even better than in the pictures. We ran inside to find our bedrooms. The kids each had their own, and Eric and I had the master suite. The whole side of the house that was facing the ocean was covered with windows. The water was right outside our doors, and you could hear the waves crashing from every room inside.

Our first day was spent making sandcastles on the beach and walking to the ice cream shop, which was just a couple of blocks away. This was just how I imagined our first family vacation would be. We went to bed that night with plans of doing more of the same the next day. Brynn seemed a little sick, but it wouldn't be fair for her to be sick on vacation, so I didn't put much thought into it.

A little after midnight, Eric woke me up. He said Brynn was really hot and he was sure she had a fever. The nearest store we knew of that would be open at midnight was almost an hour away. I sat in the living room with Brynn while Eric went to get medicine.

She was superhot. We didn't have a thermometer, but it was obvious she had a fever. She was in good spirits, though, so we sat there talking and laughing while waiting for Eric.

All of a sudden, Brynn started moving in a weird way. I thought she was going to throw up. I picked her up and headed to the bathroom. By the time I got there, though, I could tell something else was happening. Her whole body was convulsing as her wide eyes were locked in place. Her body was stiff. *What's going on?*

I don't know how I got to my phone or even figured out how to get to the section to actually call someone, but somehow I was holding her in one arm and calling 911 with the other hand. I was screaming while telling them that something was happening to my daughter, maybe a seizure. I remember having a hard time saying the words because I was so panicked that every inhale made a loud heaving sound. They asked what my address was. To this day it doesn't make sense how I was able to tell them the address of the house without missing a beat. In my panic, I remembered it from when I Google mapped it on my phone earlier that day. I was screaming, "Hurry!"

As I was on the phone with them, her body went from stiff to limp. She completely stopped moving. Her eyes shut. I panicked and screamed to the operator, "I think she just died!"

The operator calmly told me an ambulance was on the way and asked me to try to figure out if she was still breathing. It seemed like forever, but I finally heard her take a breath. Then another. And another. The operator told me to tell her every time Brynn took a breath (I'm pretty sure it was more to calm me down and give me something to focus on). Finally, the ambulance arrived just as Eric was pulling up. He ran in asking what was going on. I told him I thought Brynn had died, but now I think it was a seizure.

Brynn and I loaded up in the ambulance, and she started to wake up. She seemed okay at this point, so the paramedics were able to talk to both Eric and me before we left for the hospital. They explained how sometimes when kids get really high fevers, their bodies have seizures to reset themselves. It was most likely what had happened, but we should take her to the hospital just to be sure. Eric had to stay at the house because Austin was still in there sleeping.

Brynn and I rode in the ambulance until we got to the hospital. She was coming around and being her cute self. She got some medicine to help with the fever and a popsicle. Eric and Austin came to get us around four in the morning, once she was cleared to leave.

While Brynn and I were at the hospital, Eric had my phone. He posted on Facebook (from my account) explaining what had happened and asking for prayers.

It was posted as if I typed that. I'm not the type to ask for prayers. I'm embarrassed that my friends think I asked them to pray for us.

Now I'm worried what people on Facebook will think of me after what just happened? How shallow. And why didn't I even think of praying during this? All of my work on trying to get close to God, and I don't even think to pray during this whole ordeal. What's wrong with me?

We got a really positive response on the Facebook post. People actually prayed for us, and it felt good. I didn't feel so alone with this. Asking for help and support wasn't something I normally did because I saw it as a weakness. Some of our friends' kids had also had febrile seizures, and it was helpful to hear their stories. Everyone's words were so encouraging, and it was nice to know other people cared about what was happening with Brynn.

Maybe it's okay to ask for help and prayers.

We tried to have fun on the rest of the vacation, but I felt traumatized. I thought Brynn had died in my arms. It was really bothering me that I forgot to ask God to help her. I walked around with a horrible feeling I couldn't shake.

I need to do a better job of asking God and other people for help.

Summer was finally here, and we were spending most days swimming in our pool. I was determined to have a relaxing summer since our winter and spring had been so hard with the miscarriages and Brynn's seizure. It was mid-June, and the kids and I were in the pool. We had been splashing around and having a great time.

Austin said he felt tired, so I made a spot for him on a lounge chair with some beach towels for blankets. I didn't think much of it until he slept for almost three hours, which was unlike him. We figured he was getting sick, so I made a bed for him in the living room. He slept the rest of the day and through the night.

He was worse the next day. I figured he was getting strep, and took him to the doctor. I remember trying to get him into the car. He was so out of it. He couldn't stay awake for the car ride and was falling asleep during the appointment. The quick strep test came back negative, and we were told to go home. If he wasn't better by the next day, we should bring him into the emergency room. I just assumed he would be okay, but he wasn't. He had been sleeping and hadn't eaten ever since the nap by the pool two days earlier.

Eric was at work, so I called my mother-in-law to come with us to the ER. Austin had a brief moment of being awake as I was getting him dressed to go. I tried to get him to eat something. He said he couldn't eat, and he was scared. I told him I felt a little scared too. We hugged each other while we both cried. Then he fell back asleep.

When we got to the ER, they ran a bunch of tests on him. He had to have blood drawn, a CT scan, and an ultrasound. I could tell this was getting serious, so I called Eric to tell him he better get here.

By this point, Austin was worn out and irritated at all of the tests. When he was awake, he was screaming and trying to roll away from the doctors. I had to take a few breaks to go outside of the room and cry in the hallway. Finally, they said it must be some virus, and they would like to keep him overnight and get him some fluids. Hopefully, he would be okay in the morning.

Austin and I were just getting tucked in to the hospital bed for the night. Eric and Brynn were there saying good night. Austin seemed to be really out of it. Then he turned to me with a look in his eyes that made him seem like he wasn't really there. He started screaming, "Mom, help! Help me, Mom!" over and over. It was like he couldn't see me.

What's happening? Doesn't he realize I'm right here?

I grabbed his face and said, "Austin, I'm right here. I'm your mom. I love you."

He calmed down for a few seconds, and then it happened again. "Help, Mom! Help me, Mom!"

I grabbed his face and said, "Austin, I'm your mom. I'm right here. I love you." I was waiting for some sort of recognition in his eyes and wasn't finding it.

Eric told the nurses what was happening and that we were scared. This was serious. He wasn't recognizing who we were. We all realized this was a bigger deal than we'd thought. An ambulance was called to take us to Children's Hospital for further testing.

As we were waiting for the ambulance, Austin's panic attacks kept coming. "Help me! Help me!" I tried to stay strong when I was with him, but eventually I needed a break. I left Austin with Eric.

Brynn and I walked down the hallway to try to find an area where we couldn't hear Austin's screams. We couldn't find one. Eventually, I broke down on the floor in the hospital hallway. Brynn and I sat there on the floor, both crying. Finally, the ambulance came.

It was just me and Austin in the ambulance. They strapped him down in the bed. He was in full panic mode, like an animal caught in a trap. I was trying to hug him and hold him down. The whole time he was screaming, "Help me, Mom! Help me!" I just kept repeating, "Austin, I'm right here. I'm your mom. I love you." It was the longest ride of my life.

We got to Children's Hospital, and they wanted to observe him. I think he was exhausted from the hour-long panic attack in the ambulance. Eric and I tried to convince the doctors to just let us take him home. We felt like everyone was scaring him, and if we could just take him home, this would all be okay. Obviously, that would have been a terrible idea, and they didn't let us do that.

They wanted to get an MRI of his brain. The problem was that every time he was woken up or moved he erupted in his attack and screamed for help until he fell back asleep. Sometimes the screams last for thirty to forty-five minutes. The doctors realized they couldn't get him to stay still for the MRI, and they told us they'd do it in the morning along with a spinal tap.

By this point it was about five in the morning. Eric's parents had Brynn, and we had called my parents to make the four-hour drive and come to the hospital the next day. We didn't get any sleep that night. We got checked in to our room. Our parents got there right away in the morning. I remember my mom walking in, expecting Austin to be excited to see her. She started talking to him and got nothing but a blank stare. It was hard to see my parents realize how bad this was.

Next, a team of doctors came in to the room. They said they had canceled other things they had planned for the morning because Austin was top priority right now. I was thankful for the help, but my son was now top priority in the neurology wing of Children's Hospital in Minneapolis. *How is this happening?*

They explained that they would sedate him so they could get the MRI and spinal tap. Austin would be gone for three hours, but Eric and I could go with to hold him until he was sedated.

The panic attacks were still happening when he was awake, although he was sleeping most of the time. It's like we were scared for him to wake up. The panic attacks zapped any ounce of energy we had mustered up while he was sleeping. They totally destroyed us. He was asleep when we wheeled his bed down to have him sedated.

I remember holding his little four-year-old body while he was getting the medicine to help him stay asleep for the MRI and spinal tap. I could feel his body go limp in my arms just as Brynn's had a couple of months prior. I sobbed. Eric and I hugged him and told him we loved him. Then they wheeled him off. Eric and I stood in the hallway, crying and hugging. We were thinking this was the last time we would see him alive.

The next three hours were the longest of my life. I sat in the corner of our hospital room with a sheet wrapped around my stomach. I was rocking myself back and forth. Both Eric's and my parents were there, but I didn't want anyone to touch or look at me. It was pretty quiet in that room. I imagined how I would react when the doctors came in to tell me that Austin had died or would be brain dead forever and never recognize us again. I figured I would throw up right away and looked for something I would puke in.

As I was looking for a place to throw up, a question crept its way into my mind. *Do I trust God?* I remember telling myself how trusting God should be easy. I just accept He has a plan and it's better than mine. That all sounded fine until it was trusting God with Austin's life.

I don't think I can do this. Please, God, anything but this. This is too hard for me. Why my son? Don't let Austin die.

Somehow, a calm came over me. *What if this is part of God's plan for Austin and my family's life? What if I decide to trust God with this, and am able use it to show myself and other people how to trust God? Maybe Austin will be mentally handicapped, but I will trust God that this is the plan for us. What if Austin dies and I have to trust God will get us through? Do I trust God even if I can't see where this is going, and it may cost us giving up control of our son's life?* I didn't have a better option. I was going to pray for guidance and trust that God would get us through, no matter what happened.

I pictured God holding my face in His hands. God was right there with me. I needed to realize that it really was true. He was with me and loved me. He was waiting to see that I recognized that this was all true. He was just waiting for me to look up and realize that He has been there all along. He wanted me to let Him into my heart and life. I felt a strong assurance that this was the time to submit to God's plan. I needed to put on my tinfoil eyes and let Him lead me through this.

The doctors finally wheeled Austin back into the room after their testing. He wasn't dead. *Thank you, God.* They determined he had something called meningoencephalitis. It was something that happened when a virus (of any kind) somehow made its way into your spinal cord, traveled up to your brain, and caused the brain to swell. Meningitis was when the lining of your brain was inflamed, and encephalitis is when the actual brain got inflamed. He had both going on, which explained the confusion.

We asked if he would ever get his brain function back. They told us that he should get some, but they couldn't be sure how much. They said most kids needed some type of physical, occupational, and speech therapy to get back to normal. He may need an aide to help him at school. He may never get certain functions back. They described it like a file cabinet where all of the files get dumped out. All of the files are still there; we just don't know if they would get put back in the right place. Now we just waited until he started waking up and saw what we had to work with.

Those next days and nights in the hospital were horrible, but thankfully his panic attacks had slowed down. We had different therapists coming in to help with movement and speech if he was awake for it. I asked him questions I was sure he would know the answer to, like what his sister's name was. At first, he didn't know. It was like he knew he should know her name, but just couldn't come up with it. It broke my heart to see him struggle and eventually give up on knowing her name.

He often woke up in the middle of the night and seemed most willing to talk during that time. We went over our daily routine of what he usually ate for breakfast and watched on TV. I talked him through a typical day to see if he was able to fill in parts of the story. The speech therapist told me that if he was having trouble with a word for me to say the beginning sounds and see if that helped him figure out what word he was looking for. Sometimes that helped; sometimes it didn't.

For the first few nights, he didn't want to be touched. His senses were overloaded, so even things like having the lights on were too much for him. Hugging him was too much stimulation for him. It was so hard for me, since Austin usually wanted to cuddle all of the time. With him being so sick, I especially wanted to be holding him constantly. It was hard not to reach out and grab him. I had to just sit and wait for him to turn to me. I couldn't force it. All I wanted was for him to reach out and ask me for a hug. I would wait there every day of my life if that's what it took.

Is this what God has been doing with me for my whole life? Waiting for me to turn to Him and recognize Him? Has God been watching me every day of my life, just waiting for the moment I would let Him in?

A few days into this, Austin reached out to hold my hand. It was the best feeling. We fell asleep together holding hands. He knew who I was and wanted me to lie with him and hold him. He was coming around. He was also starting to walk a few steps as long as Eric and

I were there to help hold him up. He couldn't walk and talk at the same time, though. All of his concentration could only go into one thing at a time. His brain was healing, but too slowly for me to feel comfortable.

It was like having a baby again. He wasn't able to say most words, he needed help sitting up and walking, and he needed to wear diapers again. It was hard to see our smart, healthy, amazing boy just fall apart in a matter of days.

During our eight days in the hospital and months in physical, occupational, and speech therapy, I kept up a private Facebook page to update people on what was happening. I was asking for specific prayers and was talking about how I was trusting God with this. Many friends had their whole churches praying for Austin, so like thousands of people. I asked for specific prayers, such as having Austin drink eight ounces of water that day, and it happened. Two pastors from our church even came to pray with me. We sat in the toy area of the hospital, as I was sobbing and they were praying. It felt good to have them there.

Finally, after eight days, we got to go home. I expected everything to feel normal when we got there, but it just made me realize even more how different Austin's behavior was. We sat by the pool. Austin loved swimming more than anything, but he wouldn't get in. He just sat and stared at the pool. I posted something saying how hard it was to have him sit there and not swim, asking if someone could please pray for him to start swimming again so we could get back to the Austin we were used to. No kidding, within two hours, he just stood up out of the blue and, without saying a word, put on his goggles and started swimming and diving for toys. This was one of our many answered prayers.

Austin made a full recovery. His personality and smarts are back. We trusted God in the dark, just like in the game tinfoil eyes. God guided us and made sure we got where we needed to go safely. We just did the best we could with the situation we had been given. I was able to have a deep faith and trust in God, not because Austin made a full recovery (which I'm extremely thankful for), but because I was willing to completely trust God with the most important thing in my life.

I now understand what Jesus meant when He talked about dying to your old life to follow Him. It means giving up your plans, dreams, and control. Submit. It means trusting God has a plan for your life that's better than your own. Looking at life in this way has changed everything.

I can't help but see the parallels of Austin's sickness and my own journey with God. It's like I was the sick one. God was waiting for me to realize how much I needed Him. It was baby steps at first, but God has been there trying to help all along. The more I lean on God and let Him help me, the more strength I have to manage life's ups and downs. It's having Someone to help lighten the heaviness of life that I had been trying to carry on my own.

I would have never wished for Austin's sickness, but I don't know of another way for me to be so broken down that I finally got the message God has been wanting me to get all along. Our family is better for it. Our life had been turned upside down, and we came out of it much better people than we began. God can take any situation and use it for good.

Romans 8:28 (KJV) says, "And we know that all things work together for good to them that love God." My family is a witness to that.

CHAPTER 8

OUT OF PLACE

Sometimes our lives have to be completely shaken up, changed, and rearranged to relocate us to the place we're meant to be.

—Unknown author

Walls were down. I was humbled. My son was on the road to recovery. I was entering my "after." I was ready to take my next steps with my walls down. *God, how do you want me to live?* I was ready to look at life with new eyes. I was ready to make real changes in my life.

My main reasons for not letting myself believe were logic and pride. I was able to satisfy the logic part. I didn't feel prideful anymore, not after what I had just gone through.

I've discovered that people have many different reasons for not wanting to believe. Some people just don't like thinking about what may happen when they die. For others, it's thinking that becoming Christian will take away their fun and their lives will become boring. Another reason is not understanding the point of it, like how is all of this really going to help? I had all of those same questions and thoughts.

I wanted to say that I "loved" God, but what did that really mean? Love Him like I love my husband? Love Him like I love my kids? My parents? The only way to find out was to try. These "next steps" at my church were the only pieces of advice that I've ever seen that actually give a plan on what to do next if you want to deepen your faith. It's just what I was looking for. I wanted to try to get closer to God, but I wasn't sure how. I decided to make myself a "human experiment" and dive in. My goal was to know what it was like to have a relationship with our invisible God. Each one of these steps was out of my comfort zone, but I pushed through and made myself try. I'm so thankful I did. Here's how it went:

Volunteering does not come naturally to me. I'm really selfish with my time. I wish I wasn't like that. Some people are so happy giving their time to others. This would be my first step in changing my life. I was going to volunteer to help others.

My negative thoughts still crept in. *Yuck. I hate the thought of volunteering, taking my precious weekend time and spending even more of it at church. I don't think volunteering will help me. I'll volunteer in the kids' area so I don't really have to talk to any adults. Babies won't notice how out of place I feel.*

I started volunteering in the baby room one day per month. I felt uncomfortable, just like I thought I would at first. We were asked to get there early enough for the all-volunteer group huddle before it got busy.

Do all of these other people know each other really well? Do they all hang out and know I don't really belong? Am I doing this right? Can people tell how uncomfortable I feel?

The huddle would start by going over the goals for the group as a whole and end with someone leading a group prayer. I cringed and hoped nobody looked at me during the prayer because I didn't want them to see how awkward it made me feel to pray in a group like that. I looked around during the prayer.

What are other people doing? They seem to be letting this prayer sink in. Looks like they're closing their eyes. Maybe I need to try that. Nope. I can't do that. I'll just try to look down. I wish I could get out of my head enough to absorb what's being said. I'll pick one part of the prayer and try to let it sink in. Nope. Sorry. Can't do it. God, I want to pray to You but need to do it in private. I hope You understand.

It was hard to get used to going to church to help other people instead of just going to hear a message for myself. I remembered being at a neighbor's barbecue on one of the first nice days of spring. If you're from Minnesota or any other state with cold winters, then you know the kind of day I'm talking about. You go for months dreaming of the day you can finally go outside without freezing. Winter seems to take forever, and then finally the day comes. The warm sun is shining on your skin just like you've been waiting for. It's the kind of day where you would do anything to stay outside. It was a day like that, and it happened to be a day I had to volunteer at church.

What? This isn't fair. I knew I shouldn't have signed up for this. Now I have to miss a beautiful day like this to go inside a dark church and watch other people's kids. I turned down a cold beer and burger and left the party early in order to get to church for my Saturday evening volunteering. I think the people I was with were surprised when I told them I was headed to church to volunteer as this was out of character for me.

I went. The other volunteers were starting to recognize me. I felt welcomed. I was feeling more comfortable with what I was doing. I was starting to realize how good it felt to help others. Families handed over their babies so they could take in the message at church. I could tell some parents were nervous to let someone else take their babies, so I tried to give them a big smile and reassure them that they could trust me to do this. I would help take care of their baby, give them a much needed hour break from being a parent, and know they were learning about Jesus.

I think something is happening to me. I feel good about helping these people. I'm happy they're at church. I hope they enjoy the message. I hope I'm helping them feel welcomed. I wonder what brought them here? Is this their first time? Do they feel uncomfortable like I did when I first started coming? I'm going to do what I can to help them want to come back. I want them to know Jesus. Something is definitely happening to me. I'm starting to care more about others. Is this how I'm supposed to be feeling? Is it working? God, are you coming into my heart?

Ok, what's next? I think I'll try reading my Bible every day. First, I need to get a Bible. I think I can just order one on Amazon.

Why? I don't understand anything it's talking about anyway so it seems like a huge waste of time. Does anyone who reads it actually understand it? It's like it's written in a different language. I guess I'll try to do it anyway.

I had to buy a few different Bibles before I got a feel for what I could understand. I'd heard the Old Testament of the Bible was harder to read, so I started with the New Testament. This is embarrassing, but I ended up reading the New Testament of the Bible made for kids (genius kids, I think—it was as advanced as I could handle). It was written in a simpler way, and I could totally follow what was going on. It's called *The Best News Ever* by Jan Harthan. I needed an overview for what was even going on in the Bible, and this helped. After that, I moved on to a version of the Bible called The Message. It included Old and New Testament, and it was still written in a more understandable way.

Something I never understood before was the layout of the Bible's New Testament (the part written after Jesus was born). The first four stories (books) of the Bible are all the same story of Jesus's life. They're told by four different men: Matthew, Mark, Luke, and John.

Just as people today can see and hear the same things, and all have different takes on it, it's the same here. You get four different stories of Jesus's life from four different points of view. Each person has his own way of telling the same story.

My favorite is Luke. He was asked by a wealthy man to write an orderly account of Jesus's life. The man had heard many stories about Jesus and wanted to get the full story of his life. Luke was a physician. He was well educated and very concerned with facts and making sure everything was precise and accurate. His style of telling a story reminds me of my husband's, which can be a little boring if you ask me. My husband is very accurate and doesn't fluff the story to make it more interesting than it really is. He is more interested in telling a factual story than an entertaining one, but when you hear it, you never have to question its accuracy. When reading the Bible, Luke's account is my favorite because that's how he tells a story as well.

I committed to reading the Bible for fifteen minutes every morning. When I need help understanding certain parts, I look them up on a YouTube site called "Read Scripture." It's a very understandable summary of the Bible story you're about to read. The author of "Read Scripture" draws pictures to go along with the story being told. Watching and hearing that before I got into a story in the Bible gave me a summary of what to expect, so it was a lot easier to follow.

If you don't know what you're reading, then why read it? It really bothered me to read a Bible story if I had no context for the people in it, their backstories, and the culture at the time. The "Read Scripture" site helped set that up for me so I could better understand what I was reading. It's crucial to know the context in order to understand what the Bible is trying to tell us.

This same author of "Read Scripture," Tim Mackie, also has a podcast called "The Bible Project." He is a self-proclaimed "history and literary nerd" who has studied the Bible, its translations, as well as the culture at the time it was written. He breaks down the words and their intended meaning so you can understand what the author is trying to say. He has a great way of simplistically telling a complex story. I love knowing the context of what I'm reading, and this helps me. If you don't know the context, you can turn different sentences in the Bible to mean whatever you want them to mean. Context is so important.

We have this stupid cat named Squeezy. She is the most annoying cat I've ever been around. For the first year of her life, she peed on my clothes. She sometimes used her litter box, but for some reason, if I left a pile of clothes somewhere, she peed on them. She also pooped in the sink of the guest bathroom. I have no idea why. I walked down the hall, smelled it, and lost it. I had to always leave the sink full of water so she wouldn't go in it to poop. I had to get closed hampers, and I always kept my closet doors shut to make sure my clothes didn't get ruined from the pee.

One day, I had a new outfit lying out on the floor that I was going to wear to work that day. I went to put it on and then smelled it. The smell was that gross cat-pee smell that never seems to leave your nose once it gets in there. She'd peed on my new outfit. I totally lost it. I had out of control rage and didn't care that my kids were watching this go down. I chased Squeezy into the corner and started screaming, "I hate you! I hate you so much! I'm done with you! I'm getting rid of you!"

If you were a neighbor overhearing that through our open windows and had no clue of the context of what was going on, you could draw many conclusions from this. You could think I'm a horrible mom to my kids and am yelling at them. You could think I'm a mean wife who is about to leave my husband. You could think I'm the world's worst cat mom, in which case, you would be right. If you don't know the context of a story, you can draw any conclusions you want.

It always bothers me when I hear someone pick one part of a verse in the Bible and choose to build their own story based around it. Just one sentence doesn't give you any context as to what the story is trying to teach you. Once I understood context, stories of the Bible took on a whole new meaning. You know that story about Jonah? Even people who didn't go to church much have probably heard the story of this guy, Jonah, who gets swallowed by a whale and survives. This was a story that I would have rolled my eyes at and then told you how stories like that made me doubt the Bible. How unrealistic.

What if I told you that it isn't just about a fish? Mackie says that if you understood the language and culture at that time, you would see that it's basically a "Saturday Night Live" type of satire that, in part, is mocking hypocritical Christians. If you listen to The Bible Project's five-part Jonah series, you'll understand it much better. There are many other messages within that story as well. It's deep and fascinating. The story of Jonah is way more complex than thinking it's just about a guy who gets swallowed by a fish.

Actually reading and understanding the Bible can help these stories seem more real and relevant. I grew up believing the story of Jonah was about a fish. Not a horrible, hypocritical prophet. Imagine what other stories in the Bible I have misunderstood. I had written most of them off as too unrealistic to believe, but once I dug in, I realized I never understood most of the stories in the first place. Understanding these stories has helped me see how brilliantly written the Bible is and how it actually is very helpful, even in today's world.

Along with Bible reading, I read a daily devotional called *Jesus Calling* by Sarah Young. There's a page for each day of the year that is a paragraph or two long. It's inspired by different verses of the Bible but written in an understandable and inviting way. It's literally like Jesus is calling or reaching out to you and giving you glimpses of what it's like to have a relationship with him. If you're confused about how to have a "relationship" with Jesus, I recommend this book. Some days I felt as if what I was reading was so specific to my situation that it was written only for me. One of my favorite pages describes hope as a golden cord connecting you to heaven. The cord keeps you in connection to God. Without the cord of hope, your journey seems uphill and impossible. With the cord of hope, your steps feel lighter. You don't have the weight of the world on your shoulders. You can cling to the cord of hope to take the pressure off yourself and get help from God.

Daily reminders like that are helpful for me to stay connected to God and show me how to do that. I kept this in my mind recently when I was having a hard day. Things were happening that were out of my control. I pictured Jesus sending down a golden cord from heaven. I imagined myself grabbing on and releasing my weight on it. I couldn't carry this problem on my own. I needed Jesus to take my problems and lift me above them, while I trusted that He would take care of me and help me get through it. The harder I pulled, the more He would help me. There are many days when I read *Jesus Calling* that I pause, look at the sky, and mouth "thank you" to Jesus for having me read the message that day.

I set my alarm for thirty minutes before everyone wakes up. I brew a cup of coffee and settle in for my reading time. In the summer, I go out on the porch while the sun is rising. As I read, I can feel the warmth of the rising sun hitting my face. I take breaks to appreciate how peaceful this time is. I'm consumed with thankfulness for everything I have and for this peaceful part of my day. In the winter, I like to get my coffee, then crawl back into bed, and read in the coziness of my blankets. It's dark on the winter mornings, and I love the small bit of light my reading lamp produces. It feels like I'm the only one up in my own tiny corner of the world. For me, morning is the time when my mind is most at peace and open to letting the messages that I'm reading sink in. I connect with God before the chaos of my day takes me away from Him.

When I first started doing this, I read while working out on our elliptical machine in the basement. It was my only chance to work out without my kids climbing on me. I didn't let myself listen to music or watch TV. I read the Bible and *Jesus Calling* and reflected on the day ahead or on things that were bothering me. This is going to sound super weird, but I imagined Jesus sitting there on the workout bench listening to my thoughts. That's how I learned to pray. I just said (in my mind) all of the things I wanted to tell Him and ask Him. I then waited in the calm and quiet to see if any ideas popped into my head or if anything jumped out at me while reading.

I feel this is one way Jesus speaks to us. In the silence, we can feel Him directing us. We need to make the time to clear our minds and actually hear Him through little signs that He gives us. It takes practice and an open mind, but once you begin to hear His voice, you'll understand what I mean and begin hearing it more and more.

I have made this a habit, and now, years later, it's my favorite part of my day. If I miss even a few days of this, I feel disconnected and empty. Daily reading and quiet time is the best way for me to connect with Jesus. It's a way of anchoring my faith. It keeps me connected and grounded. It sets the tone for my day and, therefore, my life.

I go to a large church. They encourage small groups to get a sense of community and connect with other people with the same beliefs as you. *Like a Bible study? No way. I'm not going to sit around with a bunch of women gushing about the Bible. How could anyone think*

58

that sounded fun? It sounds like canned conversations where everyone is acting like their life is perfect. No thanks.

I put this one off for a while, but eventually I joined a small group. Our church has a group finder on their website. I felt like a mom's group was going to be good for me. At least we would all have one thing in common.

I met with one of the pastors to help me find a good mom's group in my area. The pastor was so nice and welcoming. She agreed to meet me at the Starbucks next to my salon during a break in my day. We were going to talk about finding a group. I thought it was so nice that she agreed to meet me. I wasn't used to talking about church stuff in public, but it should be fine.

I went into Starbucks and saw clients from the salon there. I got my coffee and sat down with the pastor. She was asking about my day and about some stuff going on in my life. It felt good to talk to her. We talked about what to expect with a small group. At the end, she asked if she could pray for me. I thought she meant pray for me in general, so I said sure. Then she started praying out loud.

Oh, she meant now. Like here. At Starbucks? Um, okay. She started praying for me. I wanted to be thankful for this, but I felt so uncomfortable. I was hoping nobody was listening in, and didn't know that we were praying. I was trying to close my eyes, but I just kept my head down. I was looking back and forth at the clients from the salon to make sure they weren't seeing me being prayed for out loud at Starbucks. My heart was racing, and I felt a trickle of sweat coming down my back. Finally, the prayer was over.

What's wrong with me? What a nice thing for someone to do. I wish I knew what she was saying in her prayer, but I was too worried about what other people would think. Sorry, God.

I joined a small group. In the beginning, there was just two of us who got together. I felt really nervous meeting the other mom for the first time.

What am I doing here? What if she knows way more about all of this than I do and she can tell I'm out of place? I'm so much more comfortable just reading the Bible at home by myself. How is this going to help me?

As soon as we got to talking, though, I realized how nice it was to have a conversation with someone else on the same path as I was with this church stuff. Turned out she was new to all of this too. We talked about different things going on in our lives and decided to make our meetings more formal if more people decided to come. I looked forward to meeting with her. She was the only friend I had who was interested in talking about the Bible with me, and not in a fake way. We could express questions and doubts. Talking with each other was really helpful.

Eventually, other women would come join our group. Sometimes we all order the same books to read and discuss them, sort of like a book club. We've even had some wine while talking. Sometimes we watch videos on different topics, and they bring about discussions within our own lives. Other times we read and study different Bible stories and how we can apply them to our own lives. We meet once a month. Sometimes we go out to dinner together. These women have become some of my best friends and cheerleaders in my life. We have a connection that I don't have with other friends. We talk about serious topics and how God can help us through. We can talk about troubles in our lives with no judgment. We hear miraculous stories that have happened in each other's lives. I always leave feeling really encouraged and excited to meet up again.

I'm so glad I didn't listen to myself when I thought a small group would be the worst thing ever. These women are really cool, normal, smart, and successful, and now they're some of my most supportive friends. There's nothing canned or fake about them. We don't meet for potlucks in the church basement like I imagined and feared. I'm so thankful for them, and I'm happy I put my pride aside and had the courage to join a small group.

Things were going good. All of my judgments were being proven wrong. But there was no way I was doing this next thing. I was positive I could skip this one. Baptism.

I was baptized as a baby, so there's no way I have to do that again. I don't fully understand it, but it seems super weird. Besides, it's for people who were somehow convinced this was something they had to do. I can understand probably how it's meant to make you feel, and that's good enough for me. It's for people who want extra attention and want other people to clap for them. I'm not looking for that kind of attention. Also, I don't want to get wet in front of people.

We sort of accidentally showed up for a baptism service one winter. I would have skipped if I'd known it was going to be this type of service since it made me uncomfortable.

During the message, the pastor described why we do it. Believe and be baptized. It's like the mark of a clean slate. All of your past sins are washed away. You get out of the water and into a new life. It's the mark of a second chance.

I thought of all of the sinful things I had done in my past. I felt like I was actually trying to start a fresh, new way of living. Maybe this would be a good way to mark this change that was happening. I still tried to convince myself that it wasn't totally necessary for me, but by the end of the service, both my husband and I decided it was something we wanted to do.

We decided to get baptized at our church's summer baptism in the lake. I was super nervous and didn't really tell anyone about it (except for my husband's parents who came to watch with our kids). There were over a thousand other people at the lake also getting baptized. Their families were on the grass, watching and clapping. It was a beautiful day, and everyone around was filled with joy and excitement.

This is like a whole different world. Everyone is so nice and happy for everyone else. People like this really exist? And most of them seem normal when I talk to them.

Ok, it's our turn. Here we go. I'm shaking. Am I excited or nervous? Both.

Eric and I walked into the water and saw our kids waving from shore. We linked arms. As the pastors leaned us back into the water, I imagined all the sins of my past getting washed away.

I'm fighting back the tears. This is much more powerful than I expected. I came out of the water feeling refreshed, like I was officially on a new path. This marked a change for me and a chance to keep my life going in this direction. It was an amazing experience. One of the best parts was our kids hugging us afterward and looking at us like we were the coolest people in the world. I was so happy our family was headed in this direction.

I was still uncomfortable with people outside of our church knowing about my baptism. I was worried they would think I had been brainwashed into doing weird things. I eventually told my parents and sister, and they didn't really know how to react. I quickly changed the subject.

A client from the salon was at the baptism, and saw me get baptized. She told her stylist. The stylist, who is also a good friend of mine, told me her client saw me. I sheepishly looked down and said that I did get baptized. We joked that it was my deep, dark secret.

Why am I embarrassed to admit this? Baptism is supposed to be a public declaration of your faith in Jesus. And I'm embarrassed to admit it to the public. Sorry, God.

Generosity was another thing that I was told would help me feel closer to God. I was being generous with my time when I volunteered, and that felt good. Everything else that I have been doing were helping me have a relationship with God.

Being generous with my money was different, though. It's a different type of issue that I wasn't quite ready for. Something I decided to try with the kids was put twenty dollars in an envelope and stick it on someone's car, with a note telling them to have a nice day and to treat themselves. It felt really good to picture the look on their faces when they got it. It made us feel good. *Okay, this kind of giving should be good enough.*

Churches talk about tithing, which is giving 10 percent of your income to further the mission of the church. Giving twenty dollars here and there to strangers was one thing, but being generous to the church by tithing was just not going to happen.

I'm positive if I decide to do something like that, I will have to admit I've been brainwashed.

I squirmed in my seat when our church talked about money.

I can't get on board with this. How could the church take advantage of vulnerable people and convince them their life will be better if they give tons of their money to the church? I'll give ten bucks here and there to show I support them, but will not be tricked into giving them more than that. I'm too smart and financially responsible to let them take my money.

Shortly after Austin's sickness, the money topic came up again at church. Somehow, I heard it differently this time. It's about trusting God to provide for you. We learned a lot about trust and giving up control to God in the hospital. If I was willing to trust God with Austin's life, but I wasn't willing to trust Him with my money, what did that say about where money ranked in my life? Was it more important than my son's life? No.

God knew money would be one of the hardest things to let go of. We spend our whole lives trying to get more of it, so why would we give so much away? It's backward. It is. However, it's the only place in the Bible that God says, "Test me on this" (Malachi 3:10 NIV)

I decided I was going to do it. If God says, "Test me," then I will. Occasionally my doubts about God being real still crept in. I actually would have liked some more concrete proof that He is real. I believed He saved Austin, and I could feel Him in my heart, but I have no actual hard proof. What if all of this stuff would have happened anyway? I can't trust my feelings. I need facts.

I had my 10 percent set to come out on a Monday through autopay. My tithe was a weird, random number, and I didn't round it off. I wanted it to be exactly 10 percent. I liked that it was an "off" number. I felt sick to my stomach that I was really doing this.

Have I officially been brainwashed? Does this mean I'm in some sort of church cult where they convince you to give them all of your money?

Monday came, and the money came out. I wasn't thinking much

about it when I got the mail two days later. *Looks like a bunch of bills.* I sat down to pay them. I opened my CenterPoint bill, ready to pay.

Only it wasn't a bill. It was a refund check for the *exact* amount I'd just tithed two days prior. My whole body went numb. I don't remember ever getting a refund check from CenterPoint in the past. To this day, I have never gotten another one. I believe with my whole heart that this was a sign from God. Two days after my first tithe, the exact, weird, random, not-rounded-off number right there, in black-and-white, right in front of my face.

I took a picture of it right away, afraid it would vanish into thin air. I sent the picture to my husband so I could have a witness to this. He was the only one who knew I had started tithing and knew the amount. I didn't deposit the check for a couple of weeks because I loved looking at it. Part of me thought it would turn into a pile of glitter or rise up to heaven in a beam of light.

It was right there on my kitchen counter. My actual proof. Not something in my heart or mind, but on paper. I trusted God with my tithe. He said, "Test me," and I did. God knew what sort of proof I needed to see. He came through, again, in a big way.

My husband is similar to me in the area of needing proof. He started tithing a few months after I started. He was sort of guessing what his 10 percent would be. One day, he decided to sit down and figure out what the exact number would be. It ended up being fifty dollars more per month than he had been giving for the past couple of months. He changed his monthly tithe the correct amount, fifty dollars more. A few weeks into doing that, he came out to the porch and announced, "A miracle happened to me too!"

He'd gotten a letter in the mail from his student loan account. He'd had this account for fifteen years and had never gotten a letter about it. The letter said they realized that they had made a mistake in his minimum payment calculations, and he actually owed $50 less per month than he had been paying.

We couldn't believe it. Not once, but twice with the same kind of proof. The timing and numbers were crazy. I guess you could say those things were just coincidences, but seriously, what are the chances? If those weren't clear signs that we should trust God, I don't know what is.

I'm really doing it. I've gotten out of my comfort zone and it's working. I feel closer to God. I'm proud of my church and want to make a difference there. The quiet time I spend in the morning is becoming deeper and more meaningful. The Bible verses I hear are making sense. I have a group of Christian friends. I've been baptized. I feel good giving money to a cause I believe in. I'm happy to buy a seat for someone else at church, just like someone did for me. I want other people to know more about Jesus.

Someone from work told me that my jokes aren't so mean anymore. She said my jokes used to be hurtful to other people. She told me not to worry because I was still funny (whew), but not at other people's expense anymore. *I didn't even realize I was starting to get nicer. Is that because God is in my heart?*

One other "experiment" I knew I needed to try was in my music and TV choices. I heard people talk about how good the music at our church was. It was fine, I guess, but it made me uncomfortable for some reason. If I saw people at church raising up their arms while singing, it made me squirm. I didn't get it. If I listened to music on the radio and realized it was a religious song, I quickly turned it. I didn't listen to that stuff.

A friend once convinced me to listen to a Christian radio station for a month. If I still hated it, then I could just go back to what I usually listened to. I agreed, and did not like it at first. I didn't know any of the words, and it didn't seem like the type of music I would roll down the windows and sing to. I felt embarrassed if someone was in the car with me and the song was about Jesus.

A few weeks in, I let my guard down and had to admit some of these songs were good. I did realize how much better I felt to get all of these uplifting messages and songs into my head during the day. The lyrics of the songs were so positive and wholesome. They told stories of struggles and fear, and they talked about how God showed up. I was also loving the conversations and messages that the DJs had. They gave ideas on how to help other people, and told heartwarming stories. They had people call in to tell how a song inspired them, or call asking for prayers for something going on in their lives. They gave suggestions on how to positively affect someone else's life.

It was all a stark contrast with the station I usually listened to. My old station talked about celebrity gossip and who was sleeping with who, how someone overdosed on drugs or was an addict. They had people call in because they suspected their boyfriend was cheating on them and needed help figuring out what to do. I started paying attention to the lyrics of some of the songs, and I noticed how negative many were. I didn't feel positive about the world in general after listening to my old station.

Once my month was over, I didn't go back to my old station. I enjoyed the positivity I was hearing. I started feeling that way about TV shows and movies too. Everything I was watching seemed so harsh. It made me cringe. I could see how this stuff we're so used to on TV or music was actually pretty negative and divisive. The news was mostly about people picking sides, fighting, crime, and negativity. I felt worse about life after watching most of it. I realized how much I enjoyed filling my mind with stuff that was more positive.

Side note: I still watch shows and listen to music that aren't Christian. If the song "Juicy" by Biggie comes on, I just can't turn it off. I love '90s alternative radio, country music, Imagine Dragons, and rap songs from the early 2000s. I watch *Breaking Bad* and *House of Cards*, and my latest addiction is the show *Homeland*. It's not that I always avoid shows and movies that are not wholesome—it's just that I notice more.

I compare it to eating junk food. My favorites are Cool Ranch Doritos and brownies. I also love egg bake with bacon, and if you give me cheesy potatoes, I'll eat enough to feed five adults. I'm having a great time when I'm eating all of that, but eventually I feel sick from it. That's how all of my media choices started to make me feel—sick.

My month of listening to more wholesome stuff was like taking a month to eat foods that are good for me. It just takes a couple of days for my body to feel much better and healthier. It just feels better to be healthy. That's how my mind was feeling. I didn't like all of the junk I had been so used to consuming. Once I got used to a healthier mind, I didn't like the feeling I got when I started filling it up with junk again.

These things that I'm doing are filling my soul. This isn't like getting a new outfit or something where I'm filled with happiness until I wear it once or twice and then don't care about it anymore. I'm understanding what true *joy* feels like. It's in loving other people. The feeling doesn't go away. It becomes more addicting. I want to do more of it.

Is it happening? Is this what it's like to be a Christian? I can see how this can be life changing. Jesus says the greatest commandment is to love God and love others. Am I doing that? I think I am. Are other people noticing the changes I'm making? Is this what it means to let people see God through you?

CHAPTER 9

TENTS AND CAMPING

If we find ourselves with a desire that nothing in this world can satisfy, the most probable explanation is that we were made for another world.

—C. S. Lewis

So, what's the point of all of this? I had a friend once tell me that she didn't want to go to church or get into this stuff because she just couldn't see how her life or day could get better just by praying or asking God into it.

She's right. Your day isn't going to get better. God doesn't promise us good days. He promised pain and suffering in this world because this world is a sinful place. God can't force us to turn from our sins, love Him, and follow Him. True love won't force you to love; otherwise, it isn't love. So we all have the choice to do life God's way or our own way. Too many people choose their own ways, and the world reflects that. This is a sinful world. We're all sinners. Some of us try not to sin, and some of us don't care, but we all fall short on God's plan for us.

Knowing and believing God's plan for the world will actually help you gain perspective on this life, and that's extremely helpful. If you believe what Jesus teaches, then this life isn't going to be your life forever. In the scope of eternity, your time on earth is just a tiny speck.

The Bible says that we should think of our life on earth like camping. We're currently living in tents. Our real home is much better than this. We're visitors here before we get to our true home in heaven.

You know that feeling of searching for something to satisfy you, and once you think you have it, you realize it doesn't truly satisfy? It's like we're constantly searching. I believe it's because somehow we instinctively know that we aren't where we belong. We aren't at our final destination. We're still at the campsite.

I'm not much of a camper. I love nature and being outside, but not for sleeping. Why would we sleep on the ground when we could get a hotel? What's the fun in getting a terrible night's sleep and waking up with that damp feeling? Why are we going to the bathroom outside when we could have a hotel with a toilet and maybe even a hot tub? Why does that bonfire smell never go away?

The last time I went camping was in our backyard with the kids. Eric stayed inside because he's smarter than me, but I was determined to have a fun night with the kids. Eric said I should put the rain cover on the tent just in case it rained. I told him my weather app said that there was a zero percent chance of rain, and I wanted to look at the stars while falling asleep, so no, I don't need the rain cover. I brought actual mattresses from our beds into the tent. I also had all of our good down comforters. If I'm going to camp, I'm going to be comfortable.

It was going great until around two in the morning. Everyone was sleeping until I got woken up by, you guessed it, rain. At first, it was a tiny sprinkle. No big deal. *Why didn't I listen when Eric told me to put the rain cover on?* I put up with it for a while. Then the drops got bigger and came down faster. The kids woke up. We grabbed our pillows and ran inside. We all squished into a guest bed downstairs (because our mattresses were in the tent). Eric was up in our room dry and cozy. I could almost see the huge grin on his face as he heard the rain coming down.

Here's the point—camping isn't that great. Well, maybe it's fun for some people, but if that was all you had, you probably wouldn't like it. It can be fun because we know it's temporary. We know we'll get to go back to the comforts of our home eventually.

That's how we're supposed to look at this life. We're camping. We're living in tents. It's hard. Sometimes it rains. We have to understand that we aren't home yet or we'll get crushed by every storm that comes our way.

We're a football family. We all love settling in for college football on Saturdays and NFL football on Sundays. My husband used to play college football, and if you want proof, you can ask him to show you his highlight videos. We usually are forced to watch them at least once a month. We're big fans of the team he played for. We're almost always able to watch the games on TV and sometimes travel to watch them play.

That is, until we signed our kids up for hockey. Now our weekends revolve around getting them to practice and games. Eric does almost all of the work to get the kids ready and where they need to be. My job is to come along and keep my mouth shut about how much I don't want to be a hockey mom.

One Saturday, our football team was in the quarter finals. We were hoping they would win because if they made it to the championship game, we decided our family was going to fly to Texas to watch them. The quarter finals game was at 11:00 a.m. Brynn's first hockey game was at 1:00 p.m. We were only going to be able to watch half of the football game. We talked about recording it and waiting until we got home to watch the whole thing, but we couldn't do it. We kept checking the score on our phones while at the hockey game. We knew they had won by the time we got home.

We settled in to watch the second half that we had recorded. I don't know if you've ever watched a recorded game where you already knew the ending, but it's a lot less tense. Since you already know your team will win, you aren't as nervous when something bad happens. If it looks like they're losing, you just wait. It will get better. You know it will. You already know the ending.

That is how knowing Jesus will help you. If you follow him, you know the ending. You know after this life comes your true home. Heaven. This life won't seem so tense. You won't feel so let down when it seems like everything is falling apart. Your day won't get better, but your view of your day will change. You have Jesus on your team. You know the ending. Your team wins. You're living in a tent. Jesus wins, and then you finally get to go home.

What you need to do during your time in the tent is put on your tinfoil eyes and let God lead you. God has a purpose and a plan for you. He put you on this earth for a reason. He is molding you to become who He meant for you to be. "We know that God is always at work for the good of everyone who loves him" (Romans 8:28 CEV). If you trust that, you'll have less fear of the future. Your bad day won't seem so bad, because you'll realize that God is writing your story, not you. What may seem bad may turn out to be one of the best things that happened to you.

I saw a picture that demonstrated this perfectly. It was a picture of a little girl clinging to her tiny stuffed animal. Jesus was facing her with an even bigger and better stuffed animal, but it was behind his back so the little girl couldn't see it. He was reaching out to take her tiny stuffed animal. She didn't know Jesus was going to replace it with the better one; only Jesus knew that. She wouldn't let go of her tiny one and was saying, "But I love it." Jesus was trying to get her to trust Him. If she doesn't let go of the thing she *thinks* she wants, she will never get to see the *better* thing that Jesus has for her.

How often do we cling to things because we can't trust that Jesus has something better in mind for us? In the book *Anything* by Jennie Allen, she talks about how a friend once told her, "You have to thank God for the seemingly good and the seemingly bad because, really, you don't know the difference." We don't know the plan, so we don't even know what's good for us.

Have you ever wanted something so badly that now, looking back, you realize what a big mistake it would have been? Wanting something and not getting it seems bad, but you don't know what good is around the corner. God does. What seems bad may really be for your good, and what seems good may really not be good for you.

I now pray for strength to handle what comes my way. I don't believe that God only gives you what you can handle. If He did, then why would you need Him? I think He specifically gives us what we can't handle so we have the opportunity to let Him show up in our lives. I don't try to direct the outcome of my life anymore because I don't really know where my life is supposed to be headed. I will do my best with the situations I'm given. Trust God to direct your path and you'll see the benefit of having Him in your life. Proverbs 3:5–6 (NIV) says, "Trust in the Lord with all your heart and lean not on your own understanding."

Ok, so this isn't my home. I'm in a tent. I get it. But, do I really even want to go to heaven? Isn't it just like laying around on a bunch of clouds while listening to angels play harps? That sounds really boring, and I'm not sure I could do that for eternity. Maybe I'm not meant for heaven if that's what it's like.

Good news. It's not. This is going to sound a little crazy, but the Bible says Jesus is going to return and create a new heaven and a new earth. It will be how God originally intended earth to be before we wrecked it with sin. If you like sports, there will be sports. If you like fishing, there will be fishing. If you like hanging out with your friends, you'll get to do that—only it will all be better than anything our minds can come up with. We don't know how good it can get. Everyone will be kind and gentle. There will be no evil or sin. Everything will be how it was meant to be. If we believe that someday Jesus will come back and create a "new world," heaven, then that will help us get through this world we're in now.

Opposite of heaven is hell. Hell is described as anything outside of heaven. Just as heaven isn't really clouds and harps, hell isn't fire and a little red devil. Lots of those images are not meant to be taken literally.

Hell is not being in heaven, which is said to be worse than fire and a red devil. Hell is not being with God. Hell will be understanding that you've blown it and you're not in heaven. You had all the chances possible on earth to follow Jesus, and you chose not to. Hell is God giving you what you thought you wanted. Once you realize what you're missing out on, it will be torture. This is hard for me to understand, and if it's something you struggle with as well, I suggest the book *The Case for Faith* by Lee Strobel. There's a whole chapter on hell, and it was really helpful for me to get a context as to what it all means.

As I started understanding and feeling more confident in what I was learning, I started becoming bolder in talking about it. All of this was becoming such a big part of my life, so it was hard not to mention it. Talking about God and church brought up some interesting conversations at work both with clients and with my coworkers. There are certain people that I know aren't interested in talking about it, so I make sure to talk about other stuff in front of them.

One of my clients was complaining about another person. This client knew I was going to church, but I never talked much about it with her. She was going on about what was bothering her about this other person. She then added, "And she's so religious." Right away I could tell she wished she hadn't said that around me. I realized it because right after she said the word *religious*, she looked down and then tried to change the subject.

Oh no, does she think I'm religious? I don't think I am. Am I? I believe in God and Jesus, but is that what being religious is? Or is it following a bunch of rules? I eat meat on Fridays—should I stop? Is that being religious? I think it's okay if a Catholic marries a Lutheran—is that okay? Am I doing this all wrong? What does being religious even mean? Why am I offended if someone thinks I'm religious?

What I was missing was understanding the difference between religion and a relationship with Jesus. I thought if you believed in God and went to church, you were religious.

Now that I'm getting a better understanding of Christianity, I wouldn't say I'm religious at all. To me, religion is about following different rules and grouping yourself into different sections within Christianity. Jesus never talked about Catholics, Lutherans, or Baptists. He talked about having a relationship with Him and believing in God.

Throughout history, different groups of people have interpreted parts of the Bible differently, and broken off into groups. That is where all of the different religions we see now come from. These are man-made groups that happen to interpret the Bible in different ways.

I grew up "Lutheran" only because my parents happened to go to a Lutheran church. I never knew why we went there, and I'm not sure my parents even did. It's just where their parents took them. I don't know if any of us ever questioned it.

To me, being religious is about following certain rules to please God, like going to church every Sunday or praying a certain way. Jesus isn't interested in that. He wants us to have a relationship with him, not just follow rules to show we obey. You can't "earn" your way to heaven by following rules. You get the gift of heaven by following Jesus. You can experience his help and guidance in this life by having a relationship with him. It's what we were designed for.

A religious view says, "If I obey, I will be close to Jesus." A person who is in a relationship with Jesus says, "I obey *because* I feel close to Jesus." There's a big difference in the motivation for obeying.

I think of it like a school teacher. A strict teacher will have a classroom of quiet kids, but they're obeying out of fear. They're constantly afraid they will do something wrong. From the outside, the classroom looks perfect. But inside, they're behaving that way out of fear and trying to avoid punishment. That's hard to sustain.

Another classroom can be quiet and good, but it isn't out of fear. It's because they like their teacher and have a good relationship with them. The kids want to be good because they know it will make the teacher happy. They're good because they actually want to be. The class isn't drained. They like being good. They want to be there.

That's what I think of when I try to make sense of religion and relationship. In my mind, religious people are motivated by fear of failure to God. They fear punishment if they do something wrong. Or maybe they're trying to just follow certain rules that are easier for them in order to somehow make up for the sinful things they do that they don't plan to try to stop? I know someone who doesn't ever go to church, doesn't live any sort of Christian life, but refuses to eat meat at certain times of the year. I wonder if they think that makes up for not doing anything else?

It's sort of like when I joined a CrossFit Gym. It was two years ago, and I went for three months. I made sure to talk about it all of the time, so people knew I was a "CrossFitter." The truth is it was way too hard for me. I liked just *talking* about CrossFit more than I liked actually *doing* CrossFit. Eric says he thinks I've spent more time bragging about that time I did CrossFit than I actually spent working out there. Do you like how I even managed to bring it up in this book?

You can't just talk a lot about Jesus and church or do a thing or two here and there and think you have a relationship with Him. Having a relationship with Jesus is more than checking certain things off a list.

People in a relationship with Jesus are motivated by love for God. They want to go to church, read the Bible, and serve others because they realize that's what they were made to do. They enjoy it.

Religious people were a huge turn off for me before I understood that believing in God and Jesus isn't about being religious—it's about relationship. You won't burst into flames by coming to church if you haven't followed all of the rules. You don't need to be perfect. You just have to be willing to try.

For me, my morning reading time is how I made and have kept my relationship with Jesus. I also go to church and do my best to follow what the Bible says. I *want* to do it *because* of my relationship with Jesus. Doing those things are a result of the relationship.

You're in church on average for an hour a week. If that's all you do, then that's not going to change your life or anyone else's. Church should be thought of like charging your batteries for the week ahead. It's meant to give you motivation to live out the week in the way God made us. It's not meant to be somewhere you go to "make up for" the bad things you did all week. Going to church once a week but changing nothing else in your life isn't what Jesus intended church to be. Once you're in a relationship with Jesus, you start wanting to turn from your bad decisions and start making better ones. These feelings are real. God has come into your heart. It changes you. The more you let him in, the stronger these feelings are.

Finally, the God-sized hole in my heart was getting filled. With Him. With love. The more I was getting to know Him through the Bible, prayer, and teachings, the more filled and whole I felt.

Everything else can fall apart—you can feel sad, angry, or scared, but the condition of your heart will stay intact because God is there. It's like always falling down on a soft pillow. You still fall, but it hurts less. Those are the things I was feeling. It's looking at my life and knowing I'm on the winning side and get to go to heaven when my life in the tent is over.

CHAPTER 10
THROWING STONES

*The place where you feel abandoned by everyone—
is really where God has placed you. To be met by
someone—Him.*

—Unknown author

I'm interested in getting my hands on almost any book I can that involves Christianity. One of my favorite authors is Kyle Idleman. I bought his book called *gods at War*. I had no idea what it was about. I just grabbed it because he was the author.

When I started in, I realized I wasn't going to get anything out of it. He was talking about worshiping other gods. I pictured having a statue of some other god hanging up with candles around it or something. Well, at least worshiping other gods is one thing I don't have to worry about doing.

I kept reading anyway and started to realize, oh, great, I'm not as innocent in this as I thought. The book went on to describe other "gods" at war for your heart. Only it wasn't little statues. It was things like money, food, success, entertainment, and even family that are at war for the number one thing we worship instead of God. *How could it be bad to put your family ahead of God?*

I always considered myself lucky to come from such a great family. Once my sister and I moved out of the house we grew up in, my parents built a new house at the lake that we'd had a cabin on since we had been little. It was still my safe spot, and I would get there on the weekends in the summer as often as possible. My kids loved it there, and it was so fun to see them do the same activities that I did as a kid. My parents were always so excited to have us. We had so much fun, and it was a place to escape the stress of life.

My parents were my main support system. I called my mom for everything I needed. She had always been the person I could talk to about everything in my life. I even found myself calling her about things before I talked to my husband (or God). I didn't feel as though I needed a group of close friends since I had her. I was so lucky to have a family like this.

Things were getting back on track after the miscarriages and the scares with my kids. I was looking forward to getting back to "normal." I talked to my mom on the phone a few times a week.

We were getting ready for a big family trip to Mexico for my cousin's wedding. I started getting this feeling that something weird was going on with my mom. She had just seemed a little off over the past couple of months. I was getting ready for work one day, and something told me to call her right away. I felt like she was holding something back and waiting to tell me until after the trip. I was scared that maybe she was going to tell me she had cancer or something. I called her and told her I had a weird feeling that something wasn't right. I was not prepared for what was to come next.

She told me that she and my dad were getting divorced. *Divorced.* I went into shock. I didn't know what to say or do.

We packed our bags and all met in Mexico the next day, just as we had planned.

I spent my time on our trip trying to have fun, but just sick about what I knew was going to happen to my family. *How can this be happening? They've been married for thirty-five years.*

Once we came home, it was out in the open. Our whole extended family knew. Everyone had an opinion and was letting me know about it.

78

My parents would be selling the lake. It was like my whole world of stability came crashing down. The lake and my family were my ultimate sources of comfort. I know God was supposed to be, but if I was honest, the familiarity of having the lake and my parents together felt more like a comfort to me. I could see them. I could physically go to the lake. I can't imagine life without these things. My mom said she thought the divorce would be easier on my sister and me now that we're adults and have our own families.

Was my whole childhood a lie? Were we ever really a happy family? What had really been going on? Are all of my memories fake?

I don't know how many people have been the adult child in a divorce, but it's hard in different ways. When you're an actual child, your parents feel the need to shelter you from some of the issues that are actually going on. I didn't get sheltered. I was hearing things from both sides that were none of my business to know about. I was supposed to count on *my parents* to be there for *me*, not the other way around.

I would go through phases of wanting to know everything that was going on, and then wanting to know nothing of what was going on. I wanted to pretend as though I didn't even have a family. I would ask to not be in the middle, but at the same time, I wanted to know exactly what was going on. It was distracting me from my own kids and husband. I couldn't think about anything else but how terrible this all was. I couldn't understand why this was happening.

I remember the day I saw the lake house for sale online. I sobbed hysterically. I'd thought the lake would be in our family forever. I showed Eric the online sale link. He didn't know what to say. He hugged me and told me he thought it was overpriced. I think he thought that would make me feel better. It sold right away. I felt so alone. Nobody understood how hard this was.

All of the memories—gone. The sign on the wall that said Family Is Everything—meaningless. All of the visions I had of my kids growing up there—erased.

How could the people I counted on the most all of a sudden seem

like people I don't know? How am I going to tell my kids about this?
How are they going to handle it? This is not fair!

All of the work I had done with God on staying at peace, being forgiving, and trying not to judge people went out the window. My reaction to all of this was completely out of line. I had extremely harsh words for everyone, and was filled with an anger that I couldn't get control of. I sent mean emails trying to get everyone to see things my way. I was so angry at my parents, but I knew they were hurting too. I didn't care because I felt I was hurting worse. I couldn't pull out of my own anger and sadness to care about what was happening to them too.

I was so mean and judgmental. I found Bible verses to send, as though that would help. I was turning into one of those Christians who tried to make people feel guilty for their sins. I was acting in the complete opposite way of how had learned I should, and that made me feel even worse about myself.

I couldn't even talk to my mom on the phone without completely losing control of my anger, and I yelled and screamed before I hung up. I was mean to anyone who tried to defend the situation. *How can anyone try to tell me this was going to be okay?* I knew it wasn't my job to judge, but I couldn't stop myself. My anger consumed me.

I still spent my mornings trying to tune out my anger and pray for my family. It worked for a while until I heard another detail about what was going on and my anger was back, just as strong as ever.

I had to take time away from talking to my mom. The person I used to call many times per week now became someone I couldn't even talk to. She was the person I went to when I needed to talk about problems in my life. Now I felt she was my problem.

In my weakest moments, I cried to God to take away my anger. I felt as though He was stripping away at everything in my life. I pictured myself on a mountain and everything around me was falling down. I wanted God to somehow put something into my heart that would instantly take the pain away, like a magic pill or something.

I later came to understand that when you ask God to take away your anger, instead of doing it for you, He will give you an opportunity to practice not being angry. I was starting to see that this was my big chance to learn how to truly forgive, show grace, and practice being slow to anger.

I was on the mountain. All of the other "gods" around me had crumbled. Everything I thought I could count on—people liking me, my self-sufficiency, my ability to have another baby, my kids' health, and now my family—was falling down in an avalanche all around me. The only part of the mountain I had left to stand on was God. He was the one thing that would never crumble. I pictured myself standing on God's hand while everything else was falling away. Everything else in this world can let you down, but God is always there. That is what God promises.

Other gods will let you down because they weren't made to be your rock. Don't base your life on them. They aren't as strong as God. You'll be disappointed if your life is in anything but God's hands. Now I understand what it means to have God as the foundation of your life. I need to rebuild my life with Him as the foundation, not these other things.

What if God can use this horrible situation for the good, just like he did with my miscarriages, Brynn's seizure, and Austin's sickness? Is this what the Bible means when it says that God blesses those who are poor and realize their need for Him?

I have been broken down in almost every way. I have gone from being prideful and thinking I don't need God, to being poor in spirit and realizing my need for Him. *What if instead of being buried in my anger, this could help refine me and learn more about what God needs me to learn.* The word I kept hearing in my head was forgiveness. *Do I need to learn to forgive?*

I knew the answer was yes, but I wasn't ready yet. I still somehow enjoyed my anger, even though it was making me miserable. *I need to read what Jesus says about forgiveness.* I knew it was the right thing to do. I had read about these things in the past. Forgiveness was easy to read about and understand before, when I hadn't been hurting like this. Now forgiveness seemed impossible. I knew not to judge, but what was going on around me seemed so wrong. I *know I've done things that are wrong too, but this different since it's not me doing it.*

The story that kept creeping into my heart was this one. You may recognize the saying from John 8:7 (NIV): "Let any one of you who is without sin be the first to throw a stone at her." Here is where it came from.

There were these men in the Bible called Pharisees. They were so into the rules and were always happy to point a finger and show how other people weren't following them. They completely missed Jesus's message about love and forgiveness, because they were so rigid about following the rules. When reading the Bible, it's easy to not like them. They're the tattletales. They don't understand that Jesus came to show everyone that you can't get to heaven by following these rules that the Pharisees were convinced were the only way to heaven. Jesus said He Himself was the way to heaven. Follow Him and you'll be saved from your sins. Jesus died to take away our sins, because He knows it's impossible for us to live sinless lives. We need to do our best, but we all will fail. Our main job is to love each other, and He will take care of the rest. *Oh no, I'm just like the Pharisees.*

All of this talk about love and forgiveness annoyed the Pharisees. They wanted it to be all about following certain rules. That's all they understood about getting to heaven, and they were positive that their way was the right way. They rejected Jesus's messages.

The Pharisees decided to try to trick Jesus. They wanted to put him into a situation where He would have to choose between religious laws and this love He always talked about. They found a woman who was breaking moral and religious laws. She was committing adultery. They drug her out into the middle of the town where Jesus was. The penalty for what she was doing was that she should be stoned. They brought her to Jesus and told Him of her crime.

What would He do? If He forgave her, He would be wrong because her behavior obviously was not right. If He stoned her, He would be wrong because He was preaching about forgiveness. The Pharisees had Jesus right where they wanted Him.

The woman was out for all to see. She was ashamed and sure she was about to be stoned. Everyone was waiting to see what Jesus would do.

Instead of falling into the trap, Jesus had the perfect response. He told the Pharisees that whichever one of them was without sin could throw the first stone at the woman.

They stood there shocked at the response and probably ashamed as they reflected back on their own lives. Could any one of them say they were free from sin? *Can I say I'm free of sin? Do I deserve to be throwing stones at my family?* One by one, each of the men walked away. Nobody could throw it because none of them was without sin. *I'm not without sin.* Jesus told the woman she was forgiven and to turn away from her sins.

Can you imagine how the woman felt? Jesus told her she was forgiven. It didn't matter what the other men had been saying. They were sinners too. What an amazing opportunity to change her behavior. I'm sure that was a lot of motivation for her to turn her life around. I'm sure she stumbled, but Jesus would keep on forgiving her as if she hadn't sinned at all. Jesus would forgive her. She needed to turn from her sin. He would keep loving her and keep encouraging her. He would keep picking her up when she falls.

It's called grace. There's another book by Kyle Idleman that helped me understand this called *Grace Is Greater.* Grace means God forgives us and loves us even though we don't deserve it. Jesus showed grace to the woman about to be stoned. I had experienced God's grace with all of the sins from my past. I was forgiven for all of the mistakes I had made. I was now asking for forgiveness with my anger. God was with me, giving me strength and cheering me on.

If I'm comfortable receiving grace, shouldn't I also be comfortable giving it? Of course, the answer is yes. We're to try to live like Jesus. He will show grace to my parents. I need to show grace toward my parents.

After months of not talking to my mom, I finally broke down and called to apologize. It took all of the courage I had. We agreed to go to counseling together to sort out our mutual anger and disappointment. Through prayer and counseling, I have moved toward forgiveness and grace. I still have days where I can feel the anger wanting to take over, but I have made it a practice to just let it go. It's not always easy, but it's the right thing to do.

The lake house sold. My dad moved into another house. My mom has remarried and lives in a new lake house. My kids have handled it well, and we're all trying to move forward with our new normal. My relationship with my parents is different. Holidays are different. I have lost my "safe place" at the lake.

I'm realizing those things were never meant to take the place of God in my heart. I can't have the foundation of my life built of these things. If God is the foundation, I can handle life's storms. It doesn't mean they won't happen, but it does soften the blow. I can have peace in the chaos. I can be content because I have learned to lean on God even more. He is my rock. He is the one who will never leave. He stays constant, even when everything else is falling apart.

This understanding has helped with my own marriage. I used to be under the impression that your spouse was supposed to be your perfect counterpart. They would know exactly how to help you up when you're feeling down. They would know just the right thing to say at the right time. You finish each other's sentences and then laugh about how the other person knew just what you were going to say. It would be just like in the movies.

The visual picture in my head of marriage was like a shark and remora. If anyone has watched Shark Week on the Discovery Channel as often as I have, you probably have noticed those fish that swim alongside the shark as they move through the water. That is a remora. The remora eats bits of food that come off of the shark when the shark eats. The remora moves in perfect unison with the shark. It's like they have one mind. They swim together perfectly. Wherever the shark goes, the remora goes. They move as one.

That's what I thought would automatically happen when you got married. Your husband would know exactly what to do to fill in all of the gaps in your life. We would perfectly move together as one. That's how you know you're meant to be. Soul mates.

You can imagine my surprise when, on our honeymoon just a few days into our marriage, Eric watched me get attacked by a shark. Instead of saving me, he laughed and then saved himself. Well, sort of.

We were in Fiji. It was beautiful, and from the main island, we took a helicopter to a private island with only our resort on it. We stayed in one of those over-the-water huts. Parts of the floor were glass so you could see fish swimming right underneath you. We could snorkel right from our room.

We were snorkeling one day and didn't realize we had gotten pretty far from the dock. All of a sudden, while I was underwater, I heard Eric yell, *"Shark!"* At first I thought he was kidding, so I looked back at him and laughed. Then my hand bumped something. I looked down and saw this big, gray "shark" that wasn't moving when I pushed it. I got so scared, swam over to Eric, and started trying to climb on him, almost drowning him to save myself. He grabbed me and threw me away to save himself and said, "Get away from me! It's following you!"

By this point, I was in full panic mode. I had always thought that if I was in a situation like this, I would remain composed and be able to make rational decisions. Well, that didn't happen. My goggles were filled with water, and so was my snorkel. This caused me to have blurred vision and to choke on the water. I was panicked and choking. I somehow was able to swim toward the dock in the most uncoordinated swim imaginable. During my swim, I looked down into the water, and there it was, still swimming right underneath me. The shark was not scared one bit. It was trying to get me.

You would think my new husband would be super worried and maybe even try to come to my rescue. Nope. Eric was watching all of this and sort of laughing. I think he knew it wasn't really a shark and thought all of this was pretty entertaining. That is, until the shark gave up on me and turned toward him. Once he realized it, he went into full panic mode with his goggles, snorkel, and panicked swim, just like me.

We finally made it to the dock and were completely out of breath. *What in the world was that thing?* We later found out it was a remora. The small fish that follow sharks. They're about a million times bigger in real life than they look on TV. They try to attach themselves to divers, snorkelers, and other animals. This thing was trying to attach to us. That explains why it was swimming so close and not afraid. If it had attached to me, I'm pretty sure I would have died of fear. As far as I'm concerned, we survived a shark attack.

Why didn't Eric try to save me? Why did he throw his new bride to the shark to save himself? We still love that story and laugh every time we tell it, but the truth is, it isn't the only time he's let me down. I've let him down many times too. What we've learned in our marriage is that it's the opposite of what we thought it was supposed to be like. We aren't meant to complete each other. We weren't made to be the perfect counterparts to each other. We don't just naturally swim in unison like the shark and remora. We aren't made to fill voids in each other that were made for only God to fill.

It was such a relief to learn that. I was waiting around for Eric to fill my soul with this perfect love. When I felt he hadn't done that, I was let down. As soon as I let him off the hook for being responsible for my happiness, I became happier. In fact, instead of waiting for him to make me happy, I should find ways to make him happy. Marriage is asking yourself what the other person might need, not what you need. (I'm still working on this. This morning, I made myself a cup of coffee right after he asked if I could make him one too. I totally forgot about him and was sitting there sipping on my coffee as he was staring at me. I asked what his problem was, and he reminded me how just a few minutes ago I told him I would make him a cup too. I'm not good at thinking of him before myself, but I'm trying.) If you let God fill you with love, then you have enough to spill out onto the people who need it from you.

It's the same with my parents. They let me down. I'm sure I've let them down too. They weren't meant to be perfect. Neither are my friends or anyone else on this earth. Neither am I. Once I realized that, my expectations of myself and others became more realistic. I wasn't so harsh with everyone. I wasn't so hard on myself. Once again, I realized my dependence on God, and I became even closer to Him. Love, grace, and forgiveness are hard.

CHAPTER 11
PETTING THE CAT

Above all else, guard your heart, for everything you do flows from it.

—Proverbs 4:23 (NIV)

As I'm changing, I'm seeing the world with a whole new set of eyes. It's both wonderful and painful. I see people as people. I wonder what their stories are. I wonder what their doubts and fears are. I wonder if they feel alone. I wonder if they have people who love them. I wonder why some people seem so angry. I wonder how some people always seem happy, or if it's a mask for what's really going on. I wonder why some people seem so calm and content, but others don't. I wonder why I'm caring so much. I want to know how people feel about God. Why do they believe? Why don't they believe?

I can see the beauty in things that I didn't take time to notice before. I think about how big the universe is. Is it that huge to show us what God is capable of compared to how small we are? I'm noticing how perfectly we're made. Every tiny detail of how we're put together is amazing. Did God do that to show us that He cares about even the smallest details? I can see God in everything. I can't unsee Him when I look at the world.

I also am noticing more of what seems to be wrong with the world. These things are really sad to see. There's so much hate and evil in the world. Everyone seems to be divided and trying to love one group by hating another. This is so odd. Most of the solutions that are being presented to "help the world" are so obviously just adding fuel to the fire. It's hard to watch people fall into the trap and become part of the problem.

I feel this giant burden to become part of the solution, but I don't know where to start. I feel like I have been in the dark for my whole life and have now come out and can see the light. Every problem I see can be fixed if we would start doing life as God planned for us to do instead of this twisted way that we're doing it right now. I want others to see the light, but I have to be careful. Being too blunt with what I think will cause people to pull away, which is the opposite of what I want. The people I want to talk to are the very same people who don't want to hear what I have to say. This is going to be hard. How can I help people who don't want help?

I love dogs. I love them way more than I love cats. I don't understand cats. You go up to pet most dogs, and they're just so excited to get attention that they can hardly contain themselves. They love anything and everything about you and are just so happy to be with you. They spin in circles with excitement.

Then there are cats. I never know what a cat wants. If I try to pet the cat before it's ready, it'll either bite me or run away. I'll spend some time with the cat and think it's ready to be petted, so I'll go for it. Then it will run away and look back at me like I'm an idiot. Sometimes it will stick around, and I'll think it really likes me, and then all of a sudden, out of the blue, it turns, bites my hand, and runs off. *What did I do? I thought I had earned your trust and you bite me? Where is the dog?*

I feel scared and nervous every time I pet a cat. I feel scared and nervous every time I start to talk with people about God. What an uncomfortable topic.

Why do I feel a burden to talk about this? Why can't I want to talk about something easy with people, like what outfit would look best on them or how to decorate their home? Why am I burdened with the one topic that has made me the most uncomfortable for as long as I can remember?

Why do I care so much? I don't know. Something has changed inside of me. It's actually an additional piece of "proof" for God that I never anticipated or expected. I want other people to have God in their lives too. I want it so bad that I somehow am writing a whole book about it. My motivation is the satisfaction of knowing I've possibly helped someone take one step closer to having their life transformed for the better. My motivation is that I'm possibly helping my friends, family, and even strangers see how having God in their life will help them. I risk making myself look like a total fool for having these types of conversations. I put myself out there and run the risk of people judging me and thinking I've gone crazy.

It's weird. I get this huge rush when talking about it. I would imagine it's what it feels like for adrenaline junkies who are about to go skydiving. It's like I'm addicted to the fear that goes along with this. I'm so nervous to talk about this stuff, and then once I start, it feels like I'm doing exactly what I need to do. I would have never chosen for this to be my "thing," but here I am. I think this is my purpose, at least for now. I feel like I was made to talk about this, but I have to be careful with my approach.

I know what not to do. I was talking to one of those people who has always "just believed." Her first question for me was "How old were you when you got saved?" *Um, what? I don't understand this question.* I mumbled some answer that didn't make sense and kept talking to her. I was trying to tell her how I didn't understand how a person could always just believe and never question Christianity. She wasn't quite understanding what I was saying, so I let it go. She was talking to me about growing up and how she went about talking to other people about God. She told me that she and her friends approached random people and asked them if they knew about Jesus, the Lord and Savior of their life. She asked them if they had been saved. If they looked confused, she handed them a brochure inviting them to her church.

You've got to be kidding me. I tried to keep a straight face. I asked how people reacted when she did this. She said they were thankful to her for telling them. *They were totally lying and much more polite than I think I would have been.* In her mind, people were like dogs—eager to hear what she had to say and thankful that she had approached them.

Maybe that works with some people. I truly hope she helped someone find their way to God by doing that. Maybe. But my guess is it was an extremely uncomfortable situation for almost every person who was approached. I can't imagine anything more awkward and more of a turnoff.

When talking about God, I think people are like cats. They're not super excited for a random stranger to run up to them and ask them about God. Right now, though, you're the cat. I'm about to try to pet you. I have tried to help you get to know me and understand me. I hope I have earned your trust. I'm going to bring up some thoughts about how I now see things since becoming my "after." I have changed, and now I view the world in a different way. I have this burden to talk about it. I want to talk to people who don't understand it. I want you to understand.

I've let you into my life. I've let you get to know me. I'm not a stranger running up to you before you're ready. If you've read this far, it's time to hear about the "after." I want you to think about this stuff and how it could change your life for the better. I want to tell you some ways in which having Jesus in your life can make it better. Some of these things you may have come up with on your own, but give credit where credit is due. These concepts have been around for thousands of years. We were made to live in the ways I'm going to talk about. Don't give credit to yourself, your therapist, your friend, or your Pinterest quote board for these ideas. These are ways that God says to do life. It's not meant to be cross-stitched onto a pillow or written on a bookmark. Life is meant to be lived carefully.

Proverbs 4:23–27 (NCV) says, "Be careful what you think, because your thoughts ruin your life. Don't use your mouth to tell lies; don't ever say things that are not true. Keep your eyes focused on what's right, and look straight ahead to what's good. Be careful what you do, and always do what's right. Don't turn off the road of goodness; keep away from evil paths."

Remember: I'm not trying to tell you what to do, as if I'm doing it perfectly. I'm in the process of becoming these things too. You're the cat. This is good for you. Don't run away. Don't bite me. Keep reading. Just sit still and let me pet you.

I was watching TV recently, and this commercial came on. It was a girl in a beautiful dress running all over town. She was looking for some guy. She eventually found him, and they made out on the street. Then she looked at the camera and asked, "What would you do for love?"

Um, what? Are you saying that running around town in a beautiful dress just to make out with this hot guy is a big sacrifice? Like nobody has done as much as you have for "love"? Do you think making out and feeling this passion is love? Is this what the world is trying to tell us love and sacrifice is?

I get that this is a commercial, and I'm not usually this uptight, but I can't stand watching it. It seems as if it's on every time I turn on the TV. I know I'm sounding like an old lady who is complaining about what "kids these days" are being taught, but it's true. The world wants you to think certain things are true that really aren't true. This perfume commercial wants you to think that if you smell this certain way, are extremely good looking, and will run around town to make out with some hot stranger on the street, then that is really doing something for love.

That couldn't be further from the truth. Love isn't passion. Love isn't about what's in it for you. True love isn't just about getting what you want. It's easy to love someone who loves you. Anyone can do that. True love is actually giving up your desires for another person.

Jesus has true love for us. It had a cost. True love died for you on a cross. True love wants you in His life. Jesus would have died for you if you were the only person on earth. That is true love. Don't listen to what the world and this commercial are telling you about love. That's not the voice you should listen to. We should listen to God's voice. How does He tell us to live?

I think part of the challenge in figuring out how we're supposed to live is that we're filling our hearts and minds up with a bunch of pointless junk. We seem to be following the crowd. We're just blindly doing what celebrities and maybe even our friends are doing, and not even questioning if it's the right thing to do. There seems to be no code of conduct. Nobody has any reason to do what they're doing besides how they feel in the moment. If anyone tries to tell them otherwise, they say, "You don't *know* me!" (I envision this with a hair flip and attitude.) We're filling our hearts with the wrong kinds of things, and then we wonder why we feel lost.

Some of the things God wants us to be aware of is the condition of our heart and mind. What kinds of things are you filling your heart and mind with? If someone looked into your heart, what would they find? Another way to think about it is to ask yourself what's flowing out of you. What types of words do you say to others? What types of places do you go? What are you listening to? What are you watching? These are clues as to what's in your heart.

When you look at your heart, do you like what you see? If you do, then great. You might want to check with your friends and family to make sure you have an accurate analysis. Sometimes it's hard to see flaws in ourselves. If you don't like what you see, at least you're being honest. Maybe it's time to make some changes.

What *do* you say to others? As the owner of a hair salon for the past twelve years, I can tell you that not everyone has something nice to say. There are certain people who come to the salon and you just know they won't be happy with anything you say or do. In fact, some people actually announce it right when they get there. They tell us that no salon has ever been able to make them happy. Sounds fun, huh?

I always wonder what's really going on in their lives. Their hair isn't going to make them happy. We could get it just exactly like the picture they show us, and it won't work. They even tell us that before we get started. Nothing will make them happy. Not the right hairstyle, perfect makeup, perfect body, perfect outfit, perfect shoes, and perfect purse. These things won't make you happy either. If you're spending your time thinking these things will, you'll waste a lot of time, effort, energy, and money just to be disappointed.

So, what are *you* saying to others? Do you walk into a salon and tell them that they can't make you happy? What do you say to your waitress? What types of words do you say to your coworkers? What about your family? What about your boss? What do you say about other people? Do people want to hear what you have to say, or do you drain them with your negativity? These are all signs of what's in your heart. Think of your words as either life giving or energy sucking. Are your words filling people up or deflating them?

I love talking to people who fill me up. They're always giving compliments and making me feel better about myself. I notice them doing it to other people too. They're encouragers. They have positive outlooks on life. I always feel better after talking to them. I want to be like that. I want my words to be uplifting. I don't want to leave people feeling drained after they talk to me. I don't want to talk badly about people behind their backs. I don't want to spread gossip. Proverbs 13:3 (GNT) says, "Be careful what you say and protect your life. A careless talker destroys himself."

Where do you *go*? Where do your feet take you? Who are you hanging out with? Are you going anywhere you know you shouldn't go? Are your feet taking you to the one place you shouldn't be? Are your feet taking you to do activities that aren't good for your heart, mind, or body? Do your feet take you straight to the person's house you know you shouldn't be at? Maybe it's the house of a friend who causes you to do the wrong things. Maybe it's to go be with a person who isn't your spouse. Maybe it's to the one place you know you shouldn't go, but you can't stop yourself. Where do your feet take you?

Do your feet get you to church? Do your feet get you places where you can find support and love that is good for you? Where are your feet walking? Proverbs 13:20 (NIV) tells us, "Walk with the wise and become wise, for a companion of fools suffers harm."

What do you let your eyes *see*? Are you looking at anything on your computer that you shouldn't be? What kind of movies do you watch? What kind of video games do you play? Are you watching people stab, shoot, or blow up other people? Are you getting immune to watching people die? What kinds of texts do you send? What kinds of texts do you get? What images do you look at? What are you letting your eyes see? It's affecting who we are.

Do you look up to make eye contact with strangers and give a little smile when they walk by? Do your eyes allow you to see people as real people, with feelings and stories just like you? Do your eyes see people in need and let you see how you can help? Proverbs 4:25 (NLT) says, "Look straight ahead, and fix your eyes on what lies before you."

What do your ears *hear*? What type of music do you listen to? Have you listened to the words? Are you getting immune to some of the negative words in the music you listen to? Do the words you hear represent the way you want to live? What kinds of conversations do you let yourself hear? Do you let yourself get sucked into gossiping about others? Are you getting used to hearing people fighting and calling each other names? Are you immune to how hearing hurtful comments come out of other people's mouths are affecting you? We get used to hearing things. We don't think they affect us, but they do. Be careful what you let your ears hear.

Are your ears hearing messages of encouragement? Are your ears listening to songs that are uplifting? Let your ears hear things that are helpful and positive. Proverbs 22:17 (NIV) says to "pay attention and turn your ear to the sayings of the wise."

What if everyone paid attention to what their mouths say, where their feet take them, what their eyes see, and what their ears hear. If we all made positive changes, how would that affect our hearts? What if we all tried to do these things God's way instead of the world's way? How much better would the world be? Why aren't we trying to do this? Are these things you could try to do to help make the world a better place? Do you think this part of God's plan will help the world?

I admittedly got too caught up in the last election. I have my opinions and was interested in seeing how it would play out if some of my ideas were put into place in the government. So I voted how I voted, and paid close attention to what was going on. Slowly but surely, day by day, my view of the world got corrupted. I was careless with what my eyes saw and what my ears were hearing. I watched the news and started to realize that I wasn't watching to gain information—I was watching for drama. I wanted to see a debate in which someone would represent "my side" and chew out someone representing the "other side." It usually turned into a big fight. I got so mad at the "other side." I justified all of this by telling myself it was my responsibility to know what's going on in the world. That's true, but was that really why I was watching this all so closely? Not usually.

My opinions on politics became easier to think about and a distraction from the real problem in the world, which I think boils down to the condition of people's hearts. We get caught up on stuff that is less important because it's easier to have an opinion on. It's easier to comment on or share a post on social media about something that we can't control, then go to bed just to be mad again the next day, than it is to actually look at our own hearts and start making changes. It's easier to write "loser" or "idiot" or worse in the comments section of a post than it is to look in the mirror and see what we should change in ourselves.

I stopped watching the divisive stuff I was watching (ok, every once in a while I watch a little—I'm not perfect). As I distanced myself from it, I realized the world around me wasn't actually as bad as it seemed on TV. When I actually had conversations with real people who thought differently than me, I realized that we weren't so different after all. It's like I got caught up in what news headlines told me about people instead of paying attention to the actual people around me.

People are more than a side. I needed to pull myself out of this mind-set. I needed to be more careful with what my eyes saw and ears heard. It's important to have opinions and care about the world around me, but in the end, the government isn't going to solve the main problems in the world. I won't let myself get sucked into the view of the world that says you have to pick a side and be unloving to the other side. I decided to be more careful with my heart and mind. I decided to try to *become* the change I was wanting to see in others. I'll still be an educated voter, but I'll do more than wait for the government to fix things. Instead of being mad about border security, I decided to sponsor a child in another country. Instead of being mad about health care, I started regularly donating to a hospital that touched my heart. Instead of watching people do good things and wishing more people in the world were good like that, I decided to go out and actually do the good things myself. Instead of complaining about business being open on holidays when I think they should close, our family saved up money in order to give our waitress a giant tip on Thanksgiving morning. Boots on the ground. Walk the walk. Whatever you want to call it. I quit just having an opinion, and decided to *be* the change.

Once I started doing that, I noticed how much better my heart felt. When I got sucked back into my old ways, my heart felt full of garbage again. It felt better when I was protecting it. "Above all else, guard your heart, for everything you do flows from it" (Proverbs 4:23 NIV).

Only God can truly help our hearts. When people turn to God and truly surrender to Him, lives will change. If groups of people did this, the world would change. People would soften. We would truly care about *doing* what's right instead of just *being* right.

A lot of people claim to follow Jesus, but they aren't acting like it. You can say you believe, but if your life and actions don't change, then what's the point? Spend your time getting to know how God wants you to live instead of proving how smart and capable you are of life on your own. Are you busy criticizing how other people live before you evaluate how you live? Matthew 7:3 (NLT) talks about what Jesus said about this. "And why worry about a speck in your friend's eye when you have a log in your own?" Do you have a log in your eye? Worry about that first. Once you're perfect, then you can start criticizing others. It's so easy to criticize others, even if we do the same thing. It's easy to excuse our behavior and not someone else's.

If I'm driving and I see someone swerving on the road, I'll guarantee they're looking at their phone. I'll drive up next to them, and sure enough, they are. I'll either honk or try to make eye contact so I can give them a dirty look. I need to teach them a lesson that this is unacceptable behavior.

Have I ever looked at my phone while driving? *Well, yes, but I make sure I'm at a stoplight. I'm just quick checking something, and it won't take long. I'm really aware of my surroundings when I drive, so it's not as big of a deal.* See what I mean? Log in my eye. We all need to stop looking at our phones in the car. I can start with stopping it myself. Pay attention to when you criticize others of something you're guilty of as well. It might be more often than you think. Fix yourself, be the example, and help others.

The way God wants us to live is pretty much the opposite of our instincts. We have to practice it. We have to read and reread what Jesus taught us about living. We need to remind ourselves of it every day.

It's too easy to follow our feelings, and not Jesus, but this will never work. Would you tell a toddler to do what feels good? No. What feels good to them is eating dishwasher detergent. What feels good for them is running out into the middle of a busy street to pick up a rock. We think we've come so far once we're adults, but we haven't. If we did what feels good at the moment, we would always overeat. We wouldn't exercise. We would drink too much. We wouldn't go to work. We would spend more money than we make. When left to follow our feelings with no moral compass, we're disasters. If we live it up in this life because we'll just die anyway, we become even more selfish.

Jesus says you have to die to your old life to gain new life. This means giving up control and giving up entitlement. We're scared to do that, but we need to stop living the lie the world tells us that says we're in control of our lives. Luke 12:22–26 (NIV) says, "Therefore I tell you, do not worry about your life, what you will eat; or about your body, what you will wear. For life is more than food, and the body more than clothes. Consider the ravens: They do not sow or reap, they have no storeroom or barn; yet God feeds them. And how much more valuable you are than birds! Who of you by worrying can add a single hour to your life? Since you cannot do this very little thing, why do you worry about the rest?"

God will make sure we have what we need. We should participate in life and do the best we can with what we have, but worrying and trying to control things that we have no control of are a waste of time.

I saw a quote on Pinterest about self-sufficiency and trying to be in control. I know it was meant to be motivating to women, but it bothered me. It said, "I'm a strong, independent and self-sufficient woman, I do *not* require instruction. I know what to do, I know how to do it and when it needs to be done." *Um, do you? You don't need any instruction? You know exactly what to do and when it needs to be done? How's that going for you?*

The women I know who have this type of attitude all look capable and successful on the outside, but are wrecks on the inside. I know this because I also used to have this attitude. No wonder we have so much anxiety. We think we need to know all of this stuff about life, and it's all on us to get it done.

If this is the message that the world is giving us, it's wrong. God made us. God knows how we should live. He's trying to tell us, but most of us aren't listening. He will make sure we have what we need. He will give us the opportunity to use Him to help us know what to do and when it needs to be done. He can't do that if we don't let Him. We don't need to be in charge of most of this stuff. How much better would your life be if you let God carry the weight of the world on His shoulders instead of trying to do it on your own? He didn't make us to carry it. We aren't strong enough. We were never meant to be. Drop the weight of the world. Trust that God's got it.

Without God, life is hard. Life is also meaningless. If we try to find meaning outside of God, it won't last. Our job is to let God lead our lives by having a relationship with Jesus. Let's find the reason we were created. Why did God put you here? There was a specific reason that God wanted you here. At this place. At this time. What's your mission? This is where you'll find your value in this world.

This is your sweet spot. This will give life meaning and purpose. This is when goodness and love will flow out of your heart. Let's find it.

CHAPTER 12

BUGS IN THE KITCHEN

You may have not gone where you intended to go, but
with God, you will end up where you're meant to be.
                                            —*Unknown author*

I saw this meme somewhere that said you know you're in your forties when you have a big box of useless cords laying around that you refuse to throw away. You don't know what they plug into, but you won't get rid of them. I laughed. This is totally my husband. He thinks I throw too much away. If it were up to him, we would have little piles of "stuff we might need someday" all over the house that we can't touch or put away. It's like he thinks if you put something in a drawer, it means you never plan on using it again and it's gone forever.

So he put all of these cords in a box, and I'm not allowed to throw them.

Whenever we need a cord that we can't find, he gets super excited and gets the box out, like maybe today is the day one of those cords will finally have a purpose. Nope. The phone cord from 1995 isn't going to help us. Let's put it back in the box because you never know.

If you don't know the purpose of these cords, they're useless. Once you find what they plug into, all of a sudden they become valuable. If I could find my phone charger right now, it would be like gold. Eric got both of us new chargers after we somehow lost all of ours. He said I'm not allowed to touch his because he knew I would lose it. I surprisingly kept my cord for almost a year. It's currently lost, so when he goes to work I have to sneak over to his charger and plug my phone in. I hope Eric has quit reading this book by now so he doesn't know that I've been using his charger.

We're all like cords, and the world is our box. We all have purposes, but if we don't know what they are, we just sit in the box and feel useless. We go around trying to plug ourselves into different things, hoping to find what we're made to do. When we don't find it, we feel useless. It can be depressing to live without a sense of purpose. How do we find what we were designed to do?

The first step is knowing what our power source is. Just like an iPhone can't plug into itself to get power, we can't either. You can't plug into yourself to sustain the power and energy you'll need to get you through life. A lot of self-help books will try to tell you how to rely on yourself, motivate yourself, and fix yourself. They're all missing the main power source, and it isn't yourself. Relying on yourself won't work for the long haul. If you've tried only relying on yourself, then you know it can't last. If you think you're doing just fine plugging into yourself as your source of power, then just wait. I'll bet you an iPhone charger that you'll run out of battery at some point.

Once you realize you need power, be careful with what you try to plug into to get power. Your power source can't be your friends, spouse, or family, because they have a limited supply as well. Your power can't be based on what people think of you, if your friend texted you back soon enough, or if your boss thinks you're doing a good job at work. Most of these things are out of your control, and if you try to base your worth and power on these things, they will let you down. You'll have a short in your cord. An iPhone can't plug into another iPhone and expect to get charge from it. It will be plugged into the wrong thing and won't work properly, just like us.

God is our ultimate power source. He designed us to depend on Him. He will sustain us and give us power to do what's next. He made us, and He is waiting for us to realize that we need to rely on Him in order to function properly.

Once we plug into Him to get our power, we can be full of charge and ready to do a job. Our job is to learn what to plug the other end into. Our job is to be the cord that God's power can flow through. Our job is to be God's "middleman" and help Him accomplish His mission *through* us.

But what are we supposed to plug into? What are we supposed to do with the other ends of our cords? Once you start looking at life like this, you'll see that God has left clues everywhere for us. God knows where we'll work best, and He wants us to discover what we're made to plug into. When we find it, we find our purposes. Finding our purpose makes this life worth living. It gives us a rush. It's where our talents and passions meet.

There are so many clues to our purpose if we know what to look for. Think of your life. What are you passionate about? What makes your heart race? What makes you laugh? What makes you cry? What issues in the world make you angry? There are online sites that can help you find your purpose. Google "Spiritual Gift Finder." They call your God-given talents your *spiritual gifts*. You fill out these questions, and it will give you your top three or so gifts that can help give you clues about your purpose. It's fun to see how we're all wired differently. We're all part of God's giant "body." We each have a specific job to do. If parts of the "body" are missing, we can't accomplish as much as we could if we had that part.

Once you find your purpose, you realize you aren't just a useless cord in a box, wondering why life has no point. There's this song that I really like. You'll be surprised to know it's not another Notorious BIG song. It's actually from the Christian station. It's called "Do Something" by Matthew West. The song talks about a person shaking their fist in the air and shouting out to God about an injustice in the world. The guy says, "God, why don't you *do* something?" Like, God, where are you? If you were really there, you would fix this problem. Then the song says that God *did* do something. He created *you*.

God created *you* to do something. Once you find it, your job is to *do* it. Share your passion and purpose with the world. You were made to do what only you can do. Ask God into your heart and have Him help fuel your passion and purpose. This is the ultimate goal and will satisfy you in a way that nothing on this earth will.

Before God was in my life, I often wondered what the point of all of this is. Everything we do is here today and gone tomorrow. We get something new, and soon the excitement wears off. We cook dinner for our families just to have to cook another one. We clean our houses, and they get dirty again. We work super hard at our jobs just to retire. We build things, and they eventually fall apart. Without God's purpose, life is meaningless. This can be depressing.

What if God actually does have specific purposes for our lives? What if we have missions on this earth that only we can accomplish? What if all of this seemingly meaningless stuff actually has significance? What if God has something bigger in mind for us than what we're doing right now? What if God isn't done with us yet?

Our kids have this game called Bugs in the Kitchen. It's a really simple game, but it reminds me of purpose. The game goes like this. There's a little battery-operated "bug." When you turn it on, it vibrates and moves around the game board. On the board are little forks, spoons, and knives set up like wall barriers. Each person has a "kitchen," which is the opening you try to get the bug to crawl into.

You take turns rolling a dice that tells you which wall you get to move—the spoon, fork, or knife. If a wall isn't open, and blocking the bug's path, the bug turns itself around and eventually finds an opening to go through. The bug doesn't stop moving if the wall is blocking it; it just eventually turns itself around until it finds another opening. If you turn the walls in the right way to direct the bug into your kitchen, you get a point.

God is moving walls for us and creating path for us to reach our purposes. We bugs go full force down the path, but the bug doesn't make the path. We wait for God to open the right doors for us to go through. If a door doesn't open, we need to accept that God has something else in mind, and go in another direction. We can't ram ourselves into a wall that isn't going to open. That will exhaust us.

It's a waste of time and energy. That wall may eventually open, but it might not be at the time we expect. We need to trust God will get us to the opening when the time is right.

As we follow the paths God has mapped out for us, doors open up, and our paths get clearer. When we follow those paths, we start to see the purposes and plans God has designed specifically for us. We get to the "kitchen" when we understand our purpose.

There's a book called *What on Earth Am I Here For?* It's a forty-day guide to help find God's purpose for you. When I first started reading it, I was doubtful, and I didn't understand how it could tell me my specific purpose. I read it anyway, and what it really taught me was how to understand where God is directing me. There are clues everywhere in your life that are guiding you down the path God has set out for you. Once you tap into that, you can see how your whole life has been a plan to get you where God wants you. Your interests, experiences, and passions are all like clues from God trying to get you onto this path. I encourage you to read it and let God get you to the place where you belong.

This whole book I just wrote is actually my story of God getting me to my purpose. The funny things, horrible things, good and bad things have all come together for me to tell my story. I don't know where this will lead, but I do know that for now, there's nothing else I'm meant to be doing. God led me here. All of the doors have opened up, and my passions mixed with motivation mixed with opportunity. The right people were put in my path. This happened. I'm open to see what's next for me. The satisfaction and excitement that this has given me is unmatched. I stay up late writing this, I wake up early writing, and I write all day when my kids are at school. I can't even stop to eat because if I'm on a role, I don't want to snap out of it. I get ideas in my head of what I want to write and can't wait to get to the computer to write it out. It's like I'm a bug, and I see this bright light. I can't keep myself away from this book.

With this in mind, this Bible verse has more meaning to me, "'For I know the plans I have for you,' declares the Lord, 'plans to

prosper you and not to harm you, plans to give you hope and a future'"
(Jeremiah 29:11 NIV). Will you let God direct your path so you can
fulfill your purpose?

I read something from *Jesus Calling* that perfectly describes this.
It describes how God is taking care of you. Every detail of your life is
under His control. Everything can fit into a pattern of good if you love
Him. Don't assume things happen randomly. What we know of the
world is the tip of the iceberg. Our human understanding is limited.
We must walk by faith and not sight.

I've come out of years of darkness. I feel I have a message to give.
Me, though? What authority do I have to give messages about God?
I'm pretty average, and I didn't grow up knowing a lot of this stuff.
Can God use someone like me? Do you ever wonder how God could
possibly use you?

Once you read the Bible, you can find people in the stories that
you can relate to. My guy is Paul. Here is an overview of his story: For
the first thirty or so years of his life, his name was Saul. He was as far
from being a Christian as you can be. In fact, he hated them. The king
during that time didn't like Christians because they said Jesus was
their true king. The king thought that if he could kill all Christians,
it would put an end to the Jesus followers and bring their focus back
to himself. Saul's job was to imprison or kill all Christians he could
find. If Christians saw Saul in town, they hid.

Why was Saul so full of hatred against Christian people? I'm not
sure, but I am sure that this hatred for Christians was helpful in his
story because once he encountered Jesus, his change was so dramatic
it couldn't be something he just made up.

One day Saul and some of his men were on their way to this town
called Damascus. All of a sudden, Saul saw this bright beam of light
coming down on the road. Then he saw Jesus come from the light.
He couldn't believe what he was seeing. He talked with Jesus while
on this road. Jesus told Saul he was going to take away his eyesight.
Saul would be blind and need his friends to lead him to the next town.
Once they're there, he was supposed to wait for some guy to find him.

So, that's what Saul did. He was now blind, going to this town, and waiting for the guy that Jesus told him would come. He was in Damascus for three days waiting. He didn't eat or drink anything while he waited.

Meanwhile, God came to another man, Ananias, in a vision and told him to find Saul, place his hands on him, and restore his sight. Ananias knew who Saul was and was scared of getting arrested, but he listened and did what God told him to do.

So Ananias found Saul, and when he placed his hands on Saul's eyes, something like scales fell from Saul's eyes. Saul could see again. Saul now believed. He got up and got baptized, just like that.

At first, people around him didn't believe that he had changed. They thought it was a trick. But once they saw how passionate he was, they knew. He changed his name to Paul and went on to be one of the most influential teachers of Christianity. He was thrown in prison many times for his beliefs, and God stepped in to help every time to make sure his message got out. In fact, Paul ended up writing much of the New Testament in the Bible.

God took the worst of the worst, a man who actually killed people for being Christians, and turned him into one of the most influential leaders of Christianity. What a perfect way to show how God can do anything.

Paul didn't burst into flames when he entered a church. God used Paul and his story to show that God doesn't care about your past. He still loves you and can use you according to His plan. You aren't out of the story yet. No matter what you've done, you can be forgiven. God has been waiting for you to turn to Him. Let Him take your life into His hands and mold you into the person you're meant to be.

Once you ask God into your life, watch out. He will flip it upside down. Your job is to trust that His ways are better than your ways. Let him speak to you. Let others see how He has changed you.

I know that God has a purpose for my life and a purpose for the pain I've gone through. I believe I was put on this earth for a reason. I believe one of those reasons is to share this story. I asked God to give me eyes to see what it means to have a relationship with Him. His method of showing me has caused me to be on the brink of losing everything important to me, and it has been terrifying. The cost is worth it, though. I have learned to give Him full control of my life, to surrender.

The trials in this life, although they seem to last forever, are so small on the scale of eternity. Hard things in this life are like little time-outs, and we're the kids. It seems like we can't get through them and that the hard times will last forever, but it's just a bump in the road when you back up and view it in the scope of forever and ever. This does not minimize the weight of the hard stuff we deal with. What happens to us is often even more than we're capable of. I believe we're pushed past our capacity of what we can handle so God can show up.

When I think about the hardest times in my life, I feel like God was looking down, probably feeling bad that I was suffering, but turning me and my life toward the path He made for me.

CHAPTER 13

CHUCKING CHAIRS

Children have never been very good at listening to their elders, but they have never failed to imitate them.

—James Baldwin

Maybe you don't believe you have a purpose. Maybe you don't care enough about yourself to make changes. Maybe you still think you're better off doing life on your own. Here is one last thing to consider—someone you love looks up to you. Don't let that person miss out on the chance to live a life of purpose.

For most of us, it's our kids who look up to us. Maybe it's a niece or nephew, neighbor, or coworker. Someone else is looking for guidance, and you could be the person they're looking up to. For me, it's my eight-year-old son, Austin, and my six-year-old daughter, Brynn.

I want my kids to be successful. Everyone wants that for their kids. I don't want them bogged down with worry. I don't want them searching for validation in things that are harmful to them. I don't want them to have anxiety about their future. I don't want them to make some of the mistakes I have made.

I mostly use my phone for the camera, texting, and my social media apps. I don't know how to use most of the other features on my phone. I can't download some of the apps I want to get because I can't remember my Apple ID and password. I actually can't remember most of my passwords for anything. I tried making a list of all of my passwords, but I forgot to update the list when I had to update my passwords. It was so frustrating to try to do things with my phone, just to have to stop because I didn't know my password. You can about imagine how pumped I was when I finally realized I could do fingerprint ID instead of typing in a code. I heard the new phones now have face recognition. I wonder if we'll tell our grandkids how back in the day we had to memorize all of these passwords if we wanted to get into our accounts. They will probably wonder how we survived.

It made me wonder how many other things my phone can do that it doesn't do just because I don't know how to do them. Wouldn't it be nice if I could have the inventor of the iPhone with me all of the time telling me how to use it best? Wouldn't the one who made the iPhone help me use it to its full potential? Why would I assume I know what the iPhone can do better than the one who created it?

That seems to be what we do with our kids if we're trying to raise them our own way instead of the way their Creator intended us to raise them. Why don't I look to God for direction in this area? How does God want us to raise our kids?

I'm know I'm not a perfect parent. I'm just trying to figure this out in the best way I know how. Everything else in my life has gotten better when I do it God's way. It would make sense that parenting would be the same. Hopefully, this doesn't end up sounding like it does when someone tells you their kid only eats organic fruits and vegetables and would never eat candy, so you just wait for the moment you see that kid eat candy and are happy when they finally do. Ha-ha. The parents were wrong. Their kid isn't as great as they think. I hope you don't read this and then just wait for my kids to majorly mess up so you can tell me that this advice is garbage. I'm sure they will mess up. I plan on that. I do want to provide for them what I think is the best possible way to succeed. Raising them is my most important job, and I want to make sure I'm doing the best I can to raise successful adults.

I have mentioned that my kids are in hockey. When they first started, they skated up to the glass and gave me a double thumbs-down because they thought it was too hard. I wanted to run onto the ice, scoop them up in my arms, run out of that cold arena, and tell them we never had to come back. My husband wouldn't let me do that. I had to sit and watch them struggle. I was on the verge of tears for most of their practices.

One thing I noticed was that when the coaches showed the kids what drills to do, the coaches were skating their best. I was annoyed. *Why are you showing them how to do this in a way that they can never duplicate? Could you maybe not do it so perfectly so they aren't let down when they can't do it as good as you? Are these coaches just showing off their skills and reliving their glory days to impress the crowd?*

Then it dawned on me. The coaches know the kids won't be able to do it as good as them, but they're showing them exactly what to strive for. Practice doesn't make perfect if you're practicing the wrong way. If you aren't following perfection, you won't reach your full potential. You'll only be as good as your leader. If the person you follow is better than you, you'll always have something better to strive for.

What about in life? I know my husband and I are the biggest influences in our kids' lives right now, but am I the perfection I want them to strive for? No. I mess up all of the time. It's hard to teach my kids not to do something if *I'm* doing it. I'm supposed to be their role model.

I obviously would never want them to throw things in a rage. I want them to calmly think things through instead of throwing a tantrum. Remember the camping story that ended with it raining on us? Here's how the day started. We didn't have a good tent, so I went to Costco to get a nice, new one. The tent I found said "two-minute set up." Nice! I usually struggle to set tents up, so I'll spend the extra money so this will be easier. We got home, and I brought the kids outside. I explained that I was going to set this tent up in two minutes. I wanted them to time me to see if I could really do it in two minutes. I didn't have time to read the instructions because I was so excited to see what it was going to look like. I felt even more pressure than usual to get this thing up fast since I was being timed.

Of course, I did it all wrong since I didn't read the instructions. The kids could tell I was getting frustrated. They looked at the stopwatch on my phone and announced that so far it had been twenty minutes. What a rip-off. I got so mad that I took a chair from our outdoor furniture set, picked it up, and then chucked it as hard as I could into the fence while screaming. The kids sat there wide eyed. My son suggested that I read the instructions. *Thanks, Captain Obvious.*

Once I read the instruction manual, I saw that there was a simple thing in the first step of the instructions that I was missing. Once I got that right, everything else was easier. I could put the tent up in three minutes. I wasted a lot of time and energy trying to put it up my own way. Why didn't I just read the manual?

Wouldn't it be nice if there was an instruction manual for parenting? Where can I possibly go to get advice and guidance on raising my kids? Maybe I could try the One who created them? Guess who that is? God. Guess what? He has instructions for me if I would just see the value in them and take the time to read and follow. Jesus is like the perfect coach that we all should strive to be like. He's the one I want my kids to look up to. I want them to know I look up to Him too. We're all trying to do life like Jesus would. He wouldn't chuck a chair into the fence.

What does God have to say about raising kids? How did Jesus do life? How can I apply this to raising my kids?

Proverbs 22:6 (BSB) says, "Train a child in the way he should go, and when he is old, he will not depart from it." So we shouldn't let them get away with behavior that we wouldn't want them to have as adults. We need to teach them how to do things so that when they're older, they have the skills they need to function as productive adults.

Eric and I lean in different directions when it comes to "training" our kids. I'm a little too easygoing, like "kids will be kids." Eric can be too harsh and not let the kids figure some things out on their own without some sort of correction. We like to think we're perfectly balanced between the two, but we aren't. My laid-back attitude of "kids will be kids" isn't going to teach them anything. It's teaching them that they can just act however they feel. As an adult, we can't just go with whatever we feel. We have to go to work. We have to pay our bills. We have to shovel snow out of our driveway when it's cold outside. Usually we don't feel like doing these things, but we do because that's part of being a responsible adult. If I need to grow my kids in the direction I want them to go, I need to have rules and boundaries.

We can't be too harsh, though. Eric is learning that our kids don't need harsh discipline. Their feelings get hurt when Eric is too harsh. They don't learn anything, and just end up avoiding him. Sometimes letting them learn for themselves from natural consequences and being there to pick up the pieces works best. Ephesians 6:4 (CSB) says, "Fathers, don't stir up anger in your children, but bring them up in the training and instruction of the Lord." So we need to discipline, but not in a way that provokes them. There's a balance we need to find.

Eric and I try to balance each other out, but not in front of the kids. If one of us sees the other parent doing something we don't like, we confront each other later that day, when the kids can't hear us. We do our best to come to some sort of agreement on how we'll handle it in the future.

When the kids were little, Eric and I both decided we were okay with spanking. I was shocked, though, when I opened the mail to see that he had ordered a "spanking paddle." *No way. I didn't agree to beat our kids.* Eric told me that if it's done in the right way, it sets clear boundaries right away. Proverbs 23:13 (NLT) says, "Don't hesitate to discipline children. A good spanking won't kill them."

Ok, I'll give Eric a chance. How are we going to use this paddle? He said we would give them one chance to stop bad behavior, and tell them the next time they did whatever bad thing they were doing, they would get a spanking. If they did the bad thing again, we would tell them it was time for a spanking. We would calmly lead them to their rooms and have them grab the spanking stick that hung on the closet.

We would have them hand it to us. If it goes as planned, the biggest part of the punishment will be the kids feeling bad for it getting to this point. We shouldn't have to even spank hard. I agreed to try, and it worked. We reserved this type of punishment for the times when they knew they shouldn't be doing something, but did it anyway. We didn't have to spank anymore by the time the kids were four. They knew to listen. They each probably got a total of ten spankings. For our kids, it ended up working. There are other situations where my softer approach works. Now that they're a little older, we can send them to their room or talk about why they're having bad behavior, and that seems to work.

We make sure to love and have fun with our kids, as long as they behave within the clear boundaries we set for them. We make mistakes. We're too harsh sometimes and too laid-back at other times. The one thing we made sure of was that we were consistent in setting clear boundaries and following through with the consequences every time.

There was one time, when Austin was four, and he went against everything we had taught him. I had a neighbor babysitting the kids at her house while I was at work. It was just for a few hours. He was being naughty, and my neighbor had him go in time-out. He got so mad that he ran all the way back to our house while she thought he was in time-out. Ten minutes later, she went to get him, and he was gone. She searched her whole house and couldn't find him. She called her sister, who was nearby, to come and look for him outside while she stayed in with the other kids.

It was January and 9 degrees outside. He grabbed his shoes, but didn't have a coat. Our house is about a fourth of a mile away, which is far for a four-year-old without a coat. He made it inside by sneaking through the fence and finding a door I must have forgotten to lock. My neighbor's sister looked all over the block for him before she realized he was totally gone. Can you imagine how horrible you would feel?

Finally, her sister decided to come to our house and see if somehow he'd made it home. She came up to our front door and could see

Austin. He was sitting on our couch. He let her in, and he said he was so mad that he'd decided to walk home. She brought him back to my neighbor's house. Eric came to pick him up and heard the story. He was shocked that Austin had done this.

At home, we talked to Austin about what could have happened to him. He could have gotten hit by a car, kidnapped, frozen outside, or fallen in the pond that connected our backyards. He said he didn't care. We asked him if he knew it was wrong to run away, and he said yes. We told him that's why he was going to get a spanking. We told him he can't be doing things that he knows are wrong. He knew better. He gave Eric the stick and got a spanking. We then had him go over to the neighbor's house to apologize. He needed to look her in the eye and say he was sorry in a clear voice. Austin did it, and then came home sobbing. We made sure this gave a clear message to him that when you knowingly break the rules, you'll pay for it. To this day, he refuses to talk about that incident. I'm confident he will never do anything like that again. We felt bad for him, but we had to follow through. That was unacceptable behavior. That was the last spanking we ever had to give him.

We try to follow through with discipline 100 percent of the time. We don't make empty threats. Sometimes we're exhausted, and it would be easier to just let it slide, but I think that would be a mistake. If we're going to grow the kids in the way we want them to go, we need to be consistent.

If my life was still chaos as it was when they were babies, I wouldn't have the energy to follow through with the discipline. I've had to learn to reserve my energy to make sure I have enough to follow through with my parenting. I've had to learn to say no to stuff that isn't as important, so I have the time and energy to do my best to raise them. I try to give our family plenty of downtime to regroup and connect, so we have time to talk about what's going on in each other's lives.

There are sometimes things I wish I could be doing socially or for myself that I've had to say no to in order to focus on raising the kids. I chose to take a pay cut and drop some hours at work in order to be home for them after school. I know the time will come where I have more time for myself, and as they're getting a little older, I'm finding that. It's nice to do things I want to do, but I try to remember that this season of life isn't about me. I'll have plenty of time for myself when the kids are older. If I put in the work now, it should make future parenting a little easier. So far, so good. They know the rules and follow them. We enjoy being with our kids because their behavior is good.

We know it will get much harder in the teen years, but we hope that setting boundaries early in their lives will help. Who knows, though? We plan to step up, follow through, and do our best to grow them in the way we want them to go.

Raising them to know Jesus will give them a moral compass in a way that they wouldn't have otherwise. Going to church helps them learn things I wouldn't have thought of teaching on my own. When they come back from church, they tell us what they've learned. They recently learned about the "fruit of the spirit." They learned that when you live according to God's plan, you'll feel love, joy, peace, patience, kindness, goodness, faithfulness, gentleness, and self-control. They learned what each of those things means and how it will help their lives.

I love that they're making friends with kids who have the same values. I believe making church a priority in our family sets the tone of how we want to live. Every week, our family gets to hear messages that help us with the week ahead. There was a series at church that helped me see that my calendar was too busy and how to prioritize my life. There was even a series on parenting. I would leave every week feeling excited to use the new things I had learned to help me become a better parent.

I try to give as many opportunities as possible to answer questions they have about life and faith. I want to be available to answer their questions so they don't get answers from their friends or other people who I don't know. I'm honest about my doubts, and the kids know how I have struggled to believe.

Some of our greatest conversations happen while driving, so I don't let them do iPad or phones or watch TV unless we're on a long trip. I have Christian music in the background, and I love when my kids know the words to the songs. The songs sometime bring up conversations. One day, my daughter said it didn't make sense to her that God doesn't have a mom. I actually have struggled with that question, and I told her that. We talked it through. Sometimes talking it through with my kids helps me understand things better too. I told my daughter that there are some things we have to accept that we won't have answers for. We can't wrap our minds around certain things, such how God doesn't have a mom and has always just been there. We just have to trust that it's true.

I don't understand how an airplane can fly, but that doesn't mean it doesn't fly. I know it does because I've experienced flying on an airplane. I know enough to know that if I'm going to fly somewhere, an airplane is the wisest choice of transportation. I can't explain how something that's thousands of pounds can float through the air, but I know someone smarter than me can explain it. I don't need to know everything about airplanes in order to experience the benefit of flying in one.

It's like that with God. We don't need all of the answers in order to believe He is there. Experiencing Him can answer in a way that can't be put into words.

Deuteronomy 6:6-9 (NIV) says, "These commandments that I give you today are to be on your hearts. Impress them on your children. Talk about them when you sit at home and when you walk along the road, when you lie down and when you get up."

Recently, my son became old enough to get baptized at our church. He remembers seeing my husband and me get baptized, and we talk about it a lot during our car conversations. I wanted to make sure he knew that he should do it for himself and not because Eric and I want him to. He said he knew that, so we signed him up. He had to talk with a couple of the pastors and tell them about his decision, and why he was choosing to get baptized. Later that day, I got an email from the pastor telling me about the conversation. She said Austin said he wants Jesus to be his savior because if He wasn't, then who else would be? He wants to be baptized to show others that he follows Jesus, and so the devil won't trick him. She said Austin has a great understanding of what faith and baptism is, especially for his age. She said we're doing an incredible job as parents.

Getting an email like that is the biggest reward. Watching Austin get baptized was a reward. He told us it was special to him, and it was like scales of bad things were falling off his body into the water. I'm so proud of him and so happy we're leading him in this direction.

Eric and I agree that the responsibility of being good parents is extremely important. I don't want to assume that their teachers, neighbors, or coaches will teach them what they need to know about life. We want that job, at least at this stage of their life. Our main way to influence is to lead by example. We need to make sure we're living lives to be proud of. If we want to make sure our kids' hearts are in the right condition, we need to make sure ours are too.

This goes back to what proverbs says about taking care of our own hearts. In addition to making sure we do the right things to take care of our hearts, we need to take care of our kids' hearts. What's the condition of our kids' hearts? What flows out of them? There's a kids' song that is called "Oh Be Careful, Little Eyes." It goes something like this:

Be careful little eyes what you see
For the Father up above is looking down in love
So, be careful little eyes what you see.
Be careful little ears, what you hear
For the Father up above is looking down in love
So, be careful little ears what you hear.

It then goes on to say be careful little tongue what you say, hands what you do, feet where you go, heart whom you trust, and mind what you think.

What do their eyes see? What's on their iPads? What types of movies do they watch? What's on their social media? What types of texts do they get? What kind of shows and commercials do their eyes see? Do their eyes see kids who are left out and try to help them? Do their eyes see us being a good example? Do their eyes see us giving them the attention they need? "Be careful, little eyes, what you see."

What do their ears hear? What music do they listen to? What types of words do they hear you say? Do they hear us gossip? Do they hear us make fun of others? Do they hear us fighting? Do they hear us telling them we love them? Do they hear us encouraging them? "Be careful, little ears, what you hear."

What do their mouths say? Do they know to say please and thank you? Do they use a respectful tone? Do they talk back to us? How do our kids talk to us? How about to their teachers? "Be careful, little mouth, what you say."

What do their hands do? Do their hands hurt themselves or others? Do they use their hands to help? "Be careful, little hands, what you do."

Where do our kids go? What kind of crowd do they hang out with? Are we making sure their feet are going to church? Are they helping others? Where do their feet take them? "Be careful, little feet, were you go."

Who do our kids trust? Do they trust people they see on YouTube? Do they trust who they see on TV? Do they trust us? Who do they look up to? "Be careful little heart who you trust."

What do their minds think about? Do they have time to reflect on their day and talk about it with you? Do they think about God? Do they think about praying? Do they have time to let their minds wander, or are their minds overstimulated with schedules and media? "Be careful, little mind, what you think."

What's the condition of our kids' hearts? Let's get them to church so they can learn what to do with their eyes, ears, tongue, hands, feet, heart, and minds. Let's get under control of these things for ourselves too. Be proud to imagine your child turning out like you someday.

Give them a chance to get to know Jesus, the ultimate role model. He was compassionate, a servant, loving, forgiving, committed, prayerful, gentle, patient, had self- control, and was humble. These are qualities we should want to see in our kids. Give your kids a chance to have a perfect coach. You can't possibly be the perfect example at all times for your kids. Don't leave it up to chance as to who your kids will look up to.

In the words of my son, "If they don't follow Jesus, then who will they follow?"

WHAT'S *YOUR* STORY?

I hope this book has opened your eyes to new ideas. Here are some stories of where different people are with their faith. As you read, I hope you're able to reflect on where you are with all of this as well. I'm just going to end this book right here. I hope you liked it. Do you have an answer for the hope that you have? What's *your* story?

> "I don't believe in God, but my parents' parents raised me in church/ religious schools. Even though I don't believe, it taught me so many values. I still pop into church once in a while. I went to college for science and history, so that's what drew me away from conventional religion. It's all about just being a good person."

> "I was raised going to church, and Sundays were my favorite day. Going through life and high school I felt like everything was 'easier' on me than it was on my friends who didn't have a faith. It was like I was able to keep a peace that they didn't know how to get. In my adult years, I started questioning things about the Bible that seemed so far-fetched. Slowly, I started getting answers. I chose to be baptized about six years ago, and it was literally a breath of fresh air. There are still

answers I don't have about the Bible. Things I still feel like can be debated. I'm always open to opinions and new ways of thinking. If I wasn't, I wouldn't have been willing to listen to the ideas that confirmed my belief in God in the first place. While some things are still unanswered, the times I have seen and felt God show up in my life are things that I don't need any proof for. It's something I can't ever explain or give statistics to—it's just something I feel and know and live in my everyday life."

"I was forced to go to church from a young age. We started out Catholic until my mom was divorced and wanted to remarry, so we switched to Lutheran. My stepfather was Episcopalian, and I was forced to go to his church also. I always thought it was so far-fetched and still, in fact, do. I believe in science, not some fictitious man in a robe with a beard who lives in the sky. Good for everyone who believes in God or religion, but it's not for me at all. I just can't wrap my head around these stories in the Bible."

"I believe in God, but I don't attend church or pray as often as I've been taught I'm supposed to do. I'm Catholic but I don't agree that you need to do these things in order for God to be there for you. God is everywhere. I attended Sunday school, got baptized/ confirmed, and so on, and I always had to go to church on Sunday. I would say I've always believed in God, but do question or wonder about some of the things in the Bible and whatnot."

———————

"My story is more of an I-do-believe. I think. I mean, I know things happen for a reason that is beyond my control, and I watch for these types of messages all the time. But is that faith? Or is it only faith if you agree not to eat meat on Friday? Because some of those rules seem really petty for a man who *created everything*. But is that the only way he believes we believe? Because he's sure asking for a lot of proof from the Catholics, and they seem to have the most faith. Or is faith like being in love? Because I thought I was in love many times in my life, but now I know I wasn't until I became a mother. I even got married, and now I realize I probably had the least amount of real love for him. Will I only zero in on true faith in God if I need it? That inherently doesn't sound like faith at all. Does it even feel the same to everyone? Or is it like when you smoke too much pot and wonder if my green is the same as your green?"

———————

"I have always believed in God and His Most Blessed Mother Mary. I came from a family of strong Catholic faith and was brought up that everything we have or do in life is a gift from above! I have also been witness to see special gifts from Jesus and in turn making my faith even stronger. My family I grew up in is still very strong in our Catholic faith and continue to try to pass this blessing onto our children. Faith to me is the most precious gift we can pass on in our family friends and world. Such peace when it's found!"

———————

"I certainly believe in God. It's religion I have an issue with. Religion is man-made—the denominations: Catholic, Lutheran, Methodist, Mormon, and so on. They're not in the Bible. When religion causes people more harm than good, that is where I have a problem. The God I know is love, and love is *love*. His love is so vast we cannot even begin to fathom it. Think about it. He gave His only son, so we could be saved by His grace. That love is, in my opinion, the greatest love there is. Why would a God who loves us that much condemn people He created in His image?

"We live in a fallen world. Our job as followers of Christ is to love. Love one another as *He* loves us. Most religions teach only to love those who follow certain rules that *they* set forth. Jesus wasn't like that. Jesus hung with the 'undesirables.' My job is to be obedient to Him and what He asks of me. He's had my back and has never let me down. Has it been easy? No way. It's been the hardest journey I've ever been on. You just have to have faith. Faith in God and faith in *yourself* that the path is the right one."

"I was raised in a Christian home, and grew up going to church and Sunday school, and I even attended a Wednesday night program that was basically girl scouts for God, so God has always been a part of my life. I never questioned His existence and just knew God was there. I got sick with a rare cancer, and without my faith, I don't know how I would have made it through. I spent many hours praying to just get through the next minute of my life and to survive the treatments.

"Then my dad got sick, and instead of turning to God for comfort, I was angry, so, so angry. How could God, who was supposed to be all about love allow this amazing man to suffer so? How could He allow all this pain to happen to my family? I cursed Him. I couldn't fathom why. But I watched my parents deal with it, and they did so with grace and faith, and through much discussion and soul searching, I came to discover that God didn't 'cause' this to happen. But rather He gives us the strength to get through and the promise that one day I will see my dad again.

"I don't just *believe* in God anymore, but I have a friendship or a different relationship of sorts with Him. He is my constant companion in times of joy and heartache, someone who loves me more than I can grasp, and to me, that is the best part."

———

"God worked his way into my heart slowly, and in hindsight, I can't quite explain how it happened. I grew up with surface-level exposure to faith. We went to a Lutheran church at Christmas sometimes, but it wasn't a

125

regular thing—and my family was really happy. It never occurred to me that I needed a personal relationship with God. I believed in God—his creation pointed to his existence loud and clear, but my impression of the Bible was that it was full of stories not meant to be taken literally, and this whole Jesus thing was just too good to be true.

"Four years ago, we started going to Eagle Brook Church. It's funny, but I'm not sure why. We kept going. The messages were so full of truth, and something about it just felt like home. I knew I was holding God at arm's length, afraid to let him in. But one morning, after attending for over a year, my heart just opened up. I surrendered and invited Jesus in. And *everything* has changed since then.

"God transformed me from the inside out, and every one of his promises has come true for me. My life is full of 'peace that transcends understanding.' He's carrying my burdens, fears, and worries for me. I feel treasured, worthy, whole, and loved. I'm eager to serve, put my pride aside, and just be the light he calls us to be. There's nothing in the universe like the gift of having a personal relationship with him—he is my companion and my guide in everything. Life is richer and full of deeper joy than I ever knew before. And the funny thing is, I, too, had sought 'proof' through historical validation of the Bible, but it was actually walking with him that opened my eyes and brought the evidence that's everywhere into focus.

"I know it's easy to get tripped up on the religion thing. It's even easy to be put off by well-meaning Christians!

It kept me away from God for a long time. But being close to him is the best thing—complete love, peace, grace, and joy. Jesus wasn't kidding when he said, "I have come that they may have life, and have it to the full" (John 10:10 NIV)."